D1086054

ACHEBE'S
THINGS FALL APART

Continuum Reader's Guides

William Blake's Poetry – Jonathan Roberts

Conrad's Heart of Darkness – Allan Simmons

Dickens's Great Expectations – Ian Brinton

Fitzgerald's The Great Gatsby – Nicolas Tredell

Sylvia Plath's Poetry – Linda Wagner-Martin

ACHEBE'S
THINGS FALL APART

A Reader's Guide

ODE OGEDE

continuum

Continuum International Publishing Group
The Tower Building   80 Maiden Lane
11 York Road   Suite 704
London   New York
SE1 7NX   NY 10038

First published 2007

British Library Cataloguing-in-Publication Data
A catalogue record for this book is available from the British Library.

ISBN – 10: 0-8264-9083-2 (hardback)
0-8264-9084-0 (paperback)
ISBN – 13: 978-08264-9083-4 (hardback)
978-08264-9084-1 (paperback)

Library of Congress Cataloging-in-Publication Data
A catalog record for this book is available from the Library of Congress.

Typeset by Servis Filmsetting Ltd, Manchester
Printed and bound in Great Britain by
MPG Books Ltd, Bodmin, Cornwall

DEDICATION

This book is gratefully dedicated to the memory of my father Ogede Ode (1907–2005). He told me it was on the way, but he did not live to hold it in his hands. In bringing his vision to pass, I have relied heavily upon the everlasting love of my beloved mother Ochuole Ode.

ACKNOWLEDGEMENTS

I am indebted to many people for much assistance: Anna Sandeman, my editor at Continuum, who not only invited me to write the book but generously offered much encouragement while the study was in progress, and Professor Isidore Okpewho, who put me in contact with her. My colleague Professor Louise Maynor supported my work by granting a semester's reduced teaching load. I have been heartened by the readiness, warmth and generosity with which my friends Professors Tom Evans, Alfredia Collins, Larry Nessly, Frances Nelson, Mary Mathew and Bob Nowell III, as well as Ode Okoh and Sylvester Oboh, have responded to my questions, shared information and given advice. I also need to acknowledge my large debts to Rebecca Simmonds, Anya Wilson, Joanna Kramer, Joanna Taylor and the other editorial staff at Continuum. Graciously, my wife Shianyisimi and our children Ochuole, Ogede and Michael have been supporting my work over the years; my debt to these family members is beyond recompense.

CONTENTS

PREFACE

Few works have ever been much more read and admired than Chinua Achebe's *Things Fall Apart* (1958). Over the last 48 years or so, *Things Fall Apart* has figured prominently in the literature of several countries. Even if he had written no other, this slim book would have single-handedly secured the place of Africa's best-known novelist in any discussion of realistic historical fiction. Unarguably one of the world's greatest works of literary craftsman-ship in the genre of fact-based fiction, *Things Fall Apart* is a heart-felt story of how change affects people's lives. A magnificent treasure trove of information, a highly suggestive and telling portrait of an era, it provides a deeper understanding of Africa at a significant period of its history and a formative time in European imperial expansion in Africa than exists in any other novel. Achebe looks into the history of Europe's encounter with Africa and discovers its origin in human ambitions and shows how equivalent passions lay in the hearts of colonial subjects. As the main purpose of this study will show, through close analysis of the rhetorical strategies used in his novel and the themes he covers, not only has Achebe fascinating and original things to say about an African society just prior to and during the nascent stage of colonial occupation in the continent, but he has also given readers a novel with an unequalled display of talent which ranks among the best works of world fiction, utilizing the pressure of recorded human events as the organizing principle of narrative structure.

Things Fall Apart can justifiably be considered the earliest novel to successfully bring together in a conglomerate many of the themes and narrative techniques that now define the genre of realistic his-torical fiction in modern African literature. It is unparalleled in its elegance, lucidity, and felicity of expression; today anyone with an idea of life in Africa either acquired it through *Things Fall Apart* or soon becomes acquainted with it, because it stands out as a novel that has unquestionably opened exceptional possibilities for the genre of realistic historical fiction to unlock a window on a fast-disappearing world. Before Achebe wrote this novel, the dominant fictional model for representing Africa did not extend far beyond stereotypical depiction of the continent as a landscape without people, a jungle inhabited by undifferentiated masses of savages. Achebe breaks away from this model, which is exemplified, most notably, by the novels of Joseph Conrad and Joyce Cary, distils the unique essence of authentic African personalities and conveys that to readers. He does so through a compelling narration that marks gender differentiation with memorably cast in-depth evocations of decision-making and reasoning power displayed in activities such as household management, personal ambition, ritual observance, conversation, public debate, play and work, and the personality differences that further manifest themselves as people go about the daily business of living in their complexly organized societies.

Prima facie beginning with an image which closely approximates the reality of an African culture as it existed at about the time Africa was being opened up to European exploration and occupation, this model makes it easier for readers to understand why the violent cultural clashes which were progressively to weaken the communalistic ethos of Africa were so massively life-altering in their effects. In *Things Fall Apart*, author Achebe is not exclusively preoccupied with this drama of cross-cultural contact. But, writing concisely and wittily, he covers just enough about a decisive moment in the long and complex history of imperialism to enhance our understanding of the earliest phases of European conquest in West Africa. Examining the problems triggered by the imposition of external control and the resulting experiences of both a public and a private nature, he reveals in comprehensive detail a range of deadly emotions – anger, anxiety, condescension, radical rage and gaping dissatisfaction, desperation, inordinate ambition, inferiority complex, traumatic fear or insecurity, male superiority syndrome, shame, grief, possessiveness, impulsiveness – alternating with isolated moments of tenderness, filial love, and male friendship and female companionship, all of which ultimately outweigh the negative passions.

By placing the cultural history of an Igbo people in the context of a struggle between order and disorder during the moment of European imperial invasion, Achebe not only vividly takes readers through the daily life of the people at a transitional period, he embarks on a delicately mapped excursion into the mind of the age, setting forth more compelling constructs of the hazards of the self-perpetuating force of ambition and desperate search for social rank within the African rural setting than hitherto presented in fiction set in Africa, both African and non-African. His double-framed yarn not only sheds fresh light on key aspects of the threatened culture of the people, providing insight into how they think of others and how they imagine themselves and their communities, but it also produces a masterful portrait of the goals and hidden assumptions that underwrote the colonial mission.

For many readers Achebe himself established the parameters within which his novels, especially *Things Fall Apart*, must be understood. The outlines of these ideas are sketched with special clarity in his early essay 'The Novelist as Teacher' (1965), in which he eloquently provides answers to many of the general questions that those interested in the novels emerging from the then new nations in Africa were asking. Chief among these were how the African novel would help to draw attention to some of the bewildering moral, ethical and political problems facing the people of the continent, whether the African writer himself or herself was going to be an imitator and fill a role commensurate with the conventional image of the Western author as an alienated figure, or if he or she would closely identify with society.

Though such large questions about the goals of narrative are never easy to tackle, Achebe would not be intimidated. So, he reminded his then newly emerging audience of readers to be aware of the significance which the art of storytelling was acquiring for his new nation, as deriving its special effect from leading the people to a larger understanding of their cultural heritage. He also made known that he personally sees his novelistic ambition as being to 'help my society regain belief in itself and put away the complexes of the years of denigration and self-abasement. And it is essentially a question of education, in the best sense of that word. Here, I think, my aims and the deepest aspirations of my society meet' (reprinted in *Morning Yet on Creation Day*, 1975: 71). He goes on to add that it is the duty of the African writer to lead 'the task of re-education and regeneration that must be done' (72). He then comments on the issue of black aesthetics, that he would be 'quite satisfied if my novels (especially the ones I set in the past) did no more than teach my readers that their past – with all its imperfections – was not one long night of savagery from which the first Europeans acting on God's behalf delivered them' (72).

Although it was not Achebe's intention in offering these remarks to make a career-defining statement but simply to make his readers think about the way in which storytelling functions as a bridge between generations and as a means of passing wisdom from the very old to the young – and back again – little could he have known at the time that he was making statements that would have the unintended consequence of permanently locking the critical reception of his work into an unchanging predetermined pattern of anthropological criticism, one that would eventually lead to a stale orthodoxy. True enough, not only have his critics taken him at his word, but they have also continued to read *Things Fall Apart*, his most influential novel, primarily for its insights into African culture and history.

One of the propositions of this guide is to show that a more rewarding approach to *Things Fall Apart* must particularly also include those dazzling storytelling resources which unconsciously first draw readers to the novel and keep them riveted to it once they begin reading it: the inventive use of language, plot, setting, imagery, narrative devices, and characterization. The first chapter of this book situates the novel in its historical and cultural contexts. Chapter 2 focuses on the novel's stylistic range (its narrative technique – use of story-within-the-story, or anecdote, proverb lore, invigorated language, focalization, and management of plot). Chapter 3 deals with the key themes of the novel, such as the use of domestic life as a trope, the image of day-to-day village life, the patterns of play and work or contest, and the seasonal cycles of events, including falling in love and marriage, the position of women in society, the idea of pre-colonial law and order, festival, ritual, government and the dispensation of justice, and the colonial penetration; Chapter 4 with the critical responses to the novel and its influence. Drawing upon the best of recent scholarship, most of the material hopes to throw new light on the novel.

One further point. This guide is mandated by my sense that readers need to be supported and guided not only better to understand but also more fully to enjoy this outstanding novel, which, more than any other, has shaped the way Africa and the literature that has emerged out of the region are viewed both within and outside it, and which thus can reasonably be considered a legitimate contender for the status of the continent's best cultural capital and pre-eminent export to the world's literary community.

CHAPTER 1

THE CONTEXTS OF ACHEBE'S WRITINGS

As might be expected, because all literature bears significant traces of its context of production, an attempt to understand both the unique texture and the achievement of *Things Fall Apart* as a landmark work of art must begin with the one singular event that placed Africa generally and the novel's more immediate Nigerian (Igbo) society specifically – the primary subjects of all Achebe's fiction – in their current states: the imposition of colonialism on Africa. This was formalized by the coming together of the empire-building European powers (Britain and Belgium, France, Germany, Portugal and Spain) to divide Africa up among themselves at the Berlin Conference of 1884–5. That event, commonly called 'the partition of Africa', was originally conceived as part of a strategy to co-ordinate the ongoing scramble among the major European powers for what was then regarded as the Dark Continent. Ironically, the attempt to mediate the conflicting claims and counter-claims over the portions of Africa that each of the major European powers wanted for exclusive commercial control quickly led to one of the most catastrophic events in the continent's history: termination of autonomy or self-rule, and transformation of traditional village life hitherto enjoyed by African peoples all over their continent.

Without doubt, a surprising aspect of the European occupation and domination of Africa is that it came about as a remote consequence of schemes brought to bear to facilitate the abolition and suppression of the slave trade. Precisely at the time Africans were beginning to enjoy the fruits of legitimate trade as natural products such as cotton, ivory, gum or copal, honey and coffee started to effectively replace human beings as the mainstay of their external economies, resulting in widespread distribution of wealth among all classes of African societies, complications arose. A combination of factors joined forces to make European powers unable to resist the idea of taking actual political control of the African continent. Not the least significant of these elements were calculations relating to how European powers could monopolize and maximize profits from this external trade with Africa, as well as ideas regarding the burden of bringing enlightenment to the dark corners of the world. Thus, the years 1892 to 1904 saw the forcible imposition of colonialism by Britain on virtually all of the areas now known as Nigeria – a region to which Britain was assigned during the partition and which it ruled until 1960, within the same period that other parts of Africa were being opened up to occupation by various other European powers.

In the view of the eminent Ghanaian historian Adu Boahen, colonial conquest was a bloody affair that took the lives of countless Africans in addition to displacing many others from their homes. But aside from its obvious brutality, colonization also unleashed other far-reaching, long-term traumatic consequences: it altered dramatically the cultural, economic, social and political climate of the continent (1987: 34–57). As one of the best historians of colonialism in Africa, Boahen is better qualified than anyone to make an informed assessment of that venture, and it has been confirmed by other commentators that we have not yet fully calculated the devastation colonization caused Africa because the effects of colonial rule are continuing.[1] Usually included among the costs are the effects of economic dispossession, cultural confusion, or mental displacement, psychological disorientation, and inferiority complexes.

In theory, the Indirect Rule system of government is generally considered to be the least malevolent form of colonial rule. But even that approach to colonial rule had a destabilizing influence on the native affairs of African peoples, despite the British colonial government's avowal to assist the overseas territories to retain and preserve their traditions. Regardless of good intentions, even Indirect Rule introduced new customs regarding education, justice, work, social ranking or status, religious observance, political authority, marriage and burial, as well as ideas of honour and selfhood that were alien. And colonization could not avoid creating standards or expectations regarding duties, obligations and affiliations between individuals and the rulers that were not only intimidating to everyone among the conquered but also especially disorienting for young subject peoples.

The subjugation of Igboland was particularly sweeping. In his

absorbing biography of Achebe, Ezenwa-Ohaeto attributes the pervasive sense of disorientation and the breadth and depth of disloca-
tions within the communities to the lethal combination of forces
with which the assault of colonization was mounted. The plot to
overthrow the old order was unveiled in such a diligent manner that,
'after several expeditions', while the violence-prone military wing of
colonial power was 'entrenching its authority over the society; the
missionaries, too, were consolidating their spiritual influence after
the efforts of their pioneers; the economy was being reordered to
reflect new commercial interests; and Western education was seen
increasingly as providing opportunities for the acquisition of power
and prestige' (Ezenwa-Ohaeto, 1997: 1).

Chinua Achebe was born in 1930 at the village of Ogidi in the then
eastern region of Nigeria, now Anambra State, and he grew up there
during this deeply troubled transitional period. He received his
primary education at St Philip's Central School, Akpakaogwe
Ogidi, then entered Government College, Umuahia, one of the most
selective schools in West Africa at the time, on a competitive Owerri
Provincial Scholarship. In 1948, he enrolled at the University
College, Ibadan, first as a medical student, and then later changed
his course of study to literature. The period saw bitter and conten-
tious developments; in the midst of revolutionary changes threatening to sweep away their native customs, a large number of Igbo
people held on tenaciously to those traditions and so 'farming and
trading remained the major occupations; there were still musicians,
hunters, blacksmiths, builders, carvers and, to a lesser extent, fisher-
men along the streams of rivers. The festivals associated with
various communities, often based on religious rites, were still held,
although the zeal of some converts to the Christian religion, and the
resistance of adherents to the old traditions, sometimes met in conflict' (Ezenwa-Ohaeto, 1997: 1).

Like many other African groups, the key experiences that the
Igbos came to associate with colonial rule were the violence, pater-
nalism and repression that attended the European 'civilizing
mission'. The attempt by the colonialists to turn Igbos into imitation
whites caused major realignments of values, leading to no small con-
sternation and cultural confusion. By reconstituting both traditional political boundaries and the bases of authority among the
Igbos, colonial rule also brought about a profound and systematic
displacement of the people's traditional systems of justice. The

action of certain minority elements within Igbo communities, who desperately hoped and yearned for integration between themselves and the occupation forces while this (to the majority) unsettling process was slowly unfolding, starkly exposed a fantasy of assimilation that reflected the contradictions of the colonial encounter: the fact that, because of internal divisions within their ranks, throughout the period of European invasion, the Igbos could not present a monolithic and unified resistance.

Ironically, while the Igbo societies' rejection of some of their members as equal human beings caused a separation between them, forcing those consigned to the sphere of the inferior to seek social uplift through pacts with the European occupation forces, what these renegade groups could not suspect was that meaningful integration (or structural assimilation) was not a realizable goal due to the fact that competitiveness would, in turn, force the dominant group to seek to preserve its advantage by depriving the conquered community of the ability to compete effectively as one unit.

So powerful is this obsession with integration among a segment of the Igbo society depicted in *Things Fall Apart*, however, that the craving itself is given concrete form in symbolic names such as those given to the novel's author, who was christened Albert Chinualumogwu Achebe. An agglomeration of familiar and unfamiliar terms based on ideas very dear to his parents, Achebe was named Albert after the husband of Queen Victoria, the then reigning monarch of England, as both a statement of his parents' assimilationist aspirations and a sign of seduction by what Achille Mbembe elsewhere has called 'the charms of majesty . . . the splendor of those exercising the trappings of authority' (2001: 110). On its part, Achebe's Igbo name Chinualumogwu ('May God fight on my behalf') expresses a prayer that reflects his parents' accommodationist outlook and faith in peaceful co-existence.

Indeed, in light of the importance attached to naming by the Igbos, the significance of Achebe's names cannot be overlooked. According to Archbishop Arinze (now Cardinal), for instance, among the Igbos, 'a person's name is chosen with care. It has meaning of its own, sometimes the names of children in a large family are a short account of the fortunes of that family: its joys and its sorrows, its hopes and its fears' (1975: 188). It bears testimony of both their devotion and the integrity of their faith that young Achebe's pioneer Christian parents encountered no obstacles bringing up their son in ways that enabled him quite early to internalize their values to the extent that he grew up with an imagination belligerently fired up to blend the old and new forces.

There's no doubt that growing up under the influence of Christian parents made him more hospitable to the idea of cultural fusion. Yet, despite young Achebe's desire to harmoniously bring Europe and Africa together, he did not hold any magic wands to wave those dreams into reality. The British colonial order dictated the direction of events, which went against both young Achebe's and his parents' wishes. So, with no silver bullets or quick fixes to offer, young Achebe's and his parents' generations helplessly witnessed the drama of accelerated social change unfolding in an opposing direction. They not only experienced the crushing legacy of foreign occupation of their homeland but also lived through the indignity of colonial subjugation and subsequent political independence without the critical conditions of true sovereignty, the requisite economic self-reliance or cultural freedom, to go with it to make political freedom authentic.

While reporting on growing up under colonial rule, many writers have attempted to downplay the suffering and pain that accompanied colonization, as if centuries of histories of colonial repression can be annihilated by assuming that they have not existed. Guinean author Camara Laye in *The African Child* (1955) and his Nigerian counterpart Cyprian Ekwensi in *People of the City* (1954) are prime examples. These writers do so, in part, because representing imperialism in all its brutality is taken by some as an attack upon the moral authority of its powerful originators, as a piece of the argument to force them to confront a political evil they would rather not acknowledge.

There are no indications that Achebe attaches slight significance to the social disruptions associated with colonialism for self-serving reasons (for example, to secure publication favours, as Laye is accused of), but this doesn't mean he couldn't have; anyone can do that without betraying his or her motives, and it's clear that plenty have. Though we cannot understand why some of his early essays like 'Named for Victoria, Queen of England' (1973) give the impression that colonialism was without major negative impacts, it is significant to note that not even that essay could entirely brush aside the havoc wreaked by colonialism because it is too stark to cover up. The only reason one can think of why Achebe would attempt to half cover up and half reveal the alienating effects of colonialism, especially the confusion and disorder external control caused in the day-to-day lives of colonized peoples who were forced to live and work within settings thoroughly poisoned by rigid imported ideas of rank and status, is to convey his fascination with the idea of Igbo and European cultures co-existing on an equal footing, a concept of cross-cultural interaction which he himself characterizes as a 'cross-roads of cultures' (1975: 119).

But his essayistic representations of the stances of the Igbo encounter with Europe as a graceful fusion of cultures convey a delight at the prospect of syncretism that was quite disproportion-ate to the historical reality of tension. 'I was born in Ogidi in Eastern Nigeria of devout Christian parents', he writes, and describes the time as distinguished by huge segregation of 'Christian and non-Christian'. He adds:

> When I was growing up I remember we tended to look down on the others. We were called in our language 'the people of the church' or 'the association of God.' The others were called . . . the heathen or even 'the people of nothing.' . . . We lived at the cross-roads of cultures. We still do today . . . On one arm of the cross, we sang hymns and read the Bible night and day. On the other, my father's brother and his family, blinded by heathenism, offered food to the idols. That was how it was supposed to be anyhow. But I knew without knowing why, that it was too simple a way to describe what was going on. Those idols and that food had a strange pull on me in spite of my being such a thorough little Christian that often at Sunday services at the height of the gran-deur of the 'Deum laudamus' I would have dreams of a mantle of gold falling on me as the choir of angels drowned our mortal song and the voice of God Himself thundered: This is my beloved son in whom I am well pleased. Yes, despite those delusions of divine destiny I was not past taking my little sister to our neighbor's house when our parents were not looking and partaking of heathen festival meals. I never found their rice and stew to have the flavor of idolatry. I was about ten then. If anyone likes to believe that I was torn by spiritual agonies or stretched on the rack of my ambivalence, he certainly may suit himself. I do not remember any undue distress. What I do remember was a fasci-nation for the ritual and the life on the other arm of the cross-

roads. And I believe two things were in my favor – that curiosity and little distance imposed between me and it by the accident of my birth. The distance becomes not a separation but a bringing together like the necessary backward step which a judicious viewer may take in order to see a canvas steadily and fully. ('Named for Victoria', reprinted in *Morning Yet On Creation Day*, 1975: 119–20)

In examining this revealing moment of autobiographical commentary, much can be said. One can begin with the matter of what has to be admitted as Achebe's apparent early alienation from the collective experience of his community.[2] That piece of information concerning the mental disposition of the person who would later become Nigeria's foremost novelist is intimated perhaps unintentionally by his disquisitions on hybridity. But the disclosure of the state of things is no less telling for all that. It reveals a calm in the face of overwhelming evidence that the concerns of colonial policy were to divide his native people into good and bad, desirable and undesirable neighbours. By instigating mutual suspicion among Igbos, colonial rule segregated them into distinct camps, making each group of native people keep its distance from the other even further. As he himself observes in this report, colonialism pathologizes human interaction. Its organizing principle of governance devolved upon a dissolution of social bonds. By arousing rival emotional impulses regarding hierarchies of class and rank that either provoked pride or social embarrassment, as the case may be, among its Igbo subjects, colonial rule aggressively kept them divided. But notice the cool, dispassionate stance adopted by the report, complete with its ironic observations and its undercurrent of humour. It is prompted by Achebe's yielding to ideals that intrigue him irresistibly: cross-cultural interaction as an opportunity for unity instead of the alienation that imperialism actually created. The conception therefore seems to smooth over the real harsh conditions of colonial rule, a negation of the overbearing attitude which shadowed the activities of British colonial officials and caused them by and large to use contact as a site of control and segregation, as a force of difference rather than of merger.

In his essay 'The Arts in Africa During the Period of Colonial Rule' (1985), leading Nigerian author and Nobel Prize winner Wole Soyinka more accurately calls the period of colonial domination in

Africa the era when 'an entire people, its social organizations, and its economic and artistic patterns became subjugated to strategies for maximum exploitation by outside interests' (539). Soyinka points out that '[d]ifferent methods of foreign control or interaction with the African populace naturally evoked or created different cultural responses from the displaced Africans'. However, he identifies 'Belgian and Portuguese colonialism, as well as British settler colonialism in East Africa' as those 'easily recognized as the most ruthless on the continent' (539).

That designation by Soyinka is a perfect fit for the cultural displacement that British colonial policies created in West Africa: just as settler colonialism in East Africa left its subjects physically displaced, so cultural imperialism left its West African victims stripped bare of their identity. That is why the image created by Achebe in 'Named for Victoria', of a near-perfectly harmonious pattern of cross-cultural encounters, is misleading. It has to be admitted that the underlying factor that gave rise to the state of unrest among colonized peoples was not just the perception that the gamut of colonial oppression was aimed at expediting the absorption of the native cultures but the alienating effects colonial policies produced.

In theory Achebe thought the shelter of his own personality from intense neurosis, due to the reasonable stability of his family, gave him an exit from the mental disequilibrium associated with the dehumanizing control of European conquest. But, in truth, that is far from being the case. Hardly any sign of freedom, in fact; the absence of guilt and inferiority he wants to portray appears more an indication that he was just too young at ten fully to comprehend the disturbed condition of colonial rule. His ambivalent expressions of contempt and 'fascination', both at the same time, for his native customs, constitute a chilling proof of the uncertainty of living in a terrifying world under the pressure of being rent apart by diametrically opposed, insular systems of meanings and values which in his naive imagination he believed were capable of reconciliation. One would be hard pressed to ignore the issue of the dichotomy that is present in that report between historical reality and Achebe's own image of it as an individual; the gap between sociological truth and an idea carried in the head by him; the separation of ontological situation and psyche; the divorce of the world as it is and how he defines it to be based on what the situation felt like for him.

As indicated by 'Named for Victoria, Queen of England', the

failure to understand, much less engage with, these highly elaborated techniques of colonial control that Achebe himself has unwittingly highlighted is stunning. It points to the underhand methods by means of which imperial values were created and transmitted. Colonization made its unsuspecting subjects no more able to think clearly than zombies would under the degrading control of another person, robbing them of the capacity to engage in any form of resistance whatsoever. Mind control was an effective instrument used by colonial rule to strip its subjects of the primary condition of their humanity. The poison by acculturation packaged and hidden behind the pull of the West, that Achebe never suspected, reveals the subtle methods by which cultural imperialism has worked: by imperceptibly conditioning the minds of its subjects toward a state of oblivion.

At least one critic has argued in favour of viewing 'Named for Victoria, Queen of England' as 'a recapturing of childhood and growing up' reflecting not 'the judgement of a youngster but the justification of an adult' (Omotoso, 1996: 8). As Kole Omotoso maintains, 'the views expressed here – that the two worlds were compatible and could live side by side – does not square with the general tone of Chinua Achebe's novels and short stories where he insists on the clash of European and African cultures and a position on which a whole species of the African novel has grown' (1996: 8). One cannot agree more. It is remarkable that the body of creative work evolving from Achebe's attempt to bring an understanding to the colonial experience has attained a good deal of greater insight and significance into the difference it presents to his parallel essayistic depictions of the same event.

Achebe has written in several genres – five novels so far: *Things Fall Apart* (1958), *No Longer at Ease* (1960), *Arrow of God* (1964), *A Man of the People* (1966) and *Anthills of the Savannah* (1987); two short story collections: *The Sacrificial Egg and Other Stories* (1962) and *Girls at War and Other Stories* (1972); a poetry volume: *Beware Soul Brother and Other Poems* (1971); three books of essays: *Morning Yet On Creation Day* (1975), *Hopes and Impediments* (1988) and *Home and Exile* (2000); a novella: *Chike and the River* (1966); and an animal fable: *How the Leopard Got His Claws* (1972).

With *Things Fall Apart*, his first novel, Achebe brings under an illuminating searchlight a crucial juncture in the history of Africa's collision with Europe and the specificity of the disruptions associated with British imperial invasions of the culture of the Igbo peoples of Nigeria. Here, the frame of the narrative is supplied by oral story-telling. It is striking that Achebe himself emphasized the way his writing began as an attempt to dispute the formidable variety of neg-ative opinions about Africa made available in his day: 'At the univer-sity', he writes in 'Named for Victoria', 'I read some appalling novels about Africa (including Joyce Cary's much praised *Mister Johnson*) and decided that the story we had to tell could not be told for us by anyone else, no matter how gifted or well-intentioned' (1975: 123).

When he came to write *Things Fall Apart*, Achebe therefore relied heavily upon a domesticated, Igbo-based, English expressive mode in order to give the subject peoples dignity by capturing the flavour of their life and speech. *Things Fall Apart* is an act of cultural retrieval, of resurrecting and recreating the subsumed culture, a task Achebe undertakes not only because of his felt sense of the disloca-tion that has occurred but also because of his discomfort with the invidious misrepresentation by foreigners of the indigenous African way of life. As Paula Berggren, quoting Achebe quoting Joyce Cary, has correctly pointed out, Achebe was particularly angered that '*Time Magazine* would call Joyce Cary's *Mister Johnson* "the best novel ever written about Africa" when Cary depicted Africa as a stagnant and impoverished culture whose "people would not know the change if time jumped back fifty thousand years. They live like mice or rats in a palace floor; all the magnificence and variety of the arts, the learning and the battles of civilization go on over their heads and they do not even imagine them"' (1997: 493).

Critical discussion often turns on the influence of the beliefs and values of Achebe's catechist father, Isiah Okafor Achebe, who grad-uated from the Teacher Training College in Awka in 1904 and is believed to have embodied the tolerance that his son eventually made his personal credo. But there is another perhaps even more determinate source, as indeed Achebe himself has disclosed in the essay 'Named for Victoria' (1975: 123), to which critics would do well to turn in order to gain a definitive understanding of the texture of Achebe's writing. That source is none other than Achebe's own mother, Janet Ileogbunam Achebe. Although she herself was an educated person (she graduated from St Monica's School in Ogbunike), it was Achebe's mother who, at an early age, exposed him to the charming world of Igbo traditional storytelling and, there-fore, who is more deserving than anyone to receive credit for having consciously helped him understand why his heritage should not be ignored, thus arguably giving definition to the preparations that were to lead on to his career.

'The folk stories my mother and elder sister told me', states Achebe in 'Named for Victoria', 'had the immemorial quality of the sky and the forests and the rivers' (1975: 123). His long-term associate Ossie Enekwe concurs that Achebe's mother sustained that folkloric interest throughout his childhood, providing him with a steady supply of riveting folktales that enriched him with vocabularies for making up stories of his own (1988: 38), all of which supports Achebe's own admission that his earliest sensibilities were enshrined in the Igbo language and storytelling tradition while growing up 'fond of stories and intrigued by language – first Igbo, spoken with such eloquence by the old men of the village, and later English which I began to learn at the age of eight' (1975: 119).[3]

The evidence is overwhelming that Achebe's formal education evaded the local experience and made no cultural accommodation of the indigenous model of learning in his early upbringing, for not only was tuition in English but the curriculum comprised primarily an intensive exposure to the major trends of European fiction. This was especially the case at the University College, Ibadan, to which he proceeded following an outstanding performance at the exclusive Government College, Umuahia. There, featuring primarily the works of Thomas Hardy, A. E. Housman, W. B. Yeats, T. S. Eliot, Ezra Pound, and J. M. Synge, the English curriculum promoted expressive modes not always compatible with the Igbo narrative traditions with which Achebe was more familiar. Hence, when he began to write, the young Achebe chose to make the African oral tradition the greatest single model for his creative writing, within which he attempted to assimilate his European-language literary inheritance that he could not entirely discountenance.

'What was the common energy that Achebe, Soyinka, Okigbo and Clark drew on? What powered the surge in literary art during the 1960s? . . . Other African universities, at Legon, Ghana, and Makerere, Uganda, had been set up simultaneously without such poetry, drama, and fiction. Why Nigeria? Why Ibadan?' Robert Wren has asked (1991: 17).

The answer is, without question, found in the fortune of a happy coincidence of an abundance of factors needed to activate the creative temper of an age: the existence of conditions that were favourable, the inspiring force of male friendship or comradeship it released, and the character of personal drive that each of the agents of the creative outpouring brought to the table. 'We were extraordinarily lucky in Ibadan really in the late '50's or even before that', Molly M. Mahood, one of the professors there at the time told Robert Wren (Wren, 1991: 23). In her account in the same interview of the unusual flowering of creative talent at Ibadan, Mahood stresses that the time was uniquely ripe for a productive use of cultural nationalism:

> There was an extremely good secondary school tradition. We got the cream. Of course that meant that we were called elitist. Perhaps we were. But it did mean we could keep up a very high standard. We got the backing of London, holding the standard firm. The infrastructure of the school is, I think, all important. Now there were very good schools who worked on building up their courses to the University. That's to say, they were, in English terms, going up to 'A' levels. And this meant that they were attracting very good staff, both expatriate and Nigerian. They were nearly all boarding schools which had of course the disadvantage that, in theory, they took people away from their own environment – de-tribalized them. But then they had the *advantage* that it de-tribalized them. They thought of themselves as Nigerians. (Wren, 1991: 23)

It is remarkable that Mahood concludes her observations by noting the role played by literature in the formation and expression at this time in the early life of the Nigerian polity of what would eventually emerge as the consciousness of a nation. Literature was, as she notes, an effective agent of 'de-tribalization, but it gave people a chance to be tribal in the sense of preserving and celebrating, as it were, their own tribal culture, and therefore they didn't need to do it to the same extent, in their own social life' (Wren, 1991: 23). Literature nourished unity in diversity, facilitating peaceful co-existence among educated Nigerians of different ethnicities; so, although 'Achebe is about as Igbo as anybody could be and I'm sure Soyinka is as Yoruba as anybody could be', Mahood says, 'they lived very happily together, Igbo, Yoruba, and the others too, as far as I could see' (Wren, 1991: 23).

John Povey offers an eloquent account of the intellectual climate prevalent at the Ibadan University College that confirms Mahood's, often helping us more clearly to understand the inevitable pressures that Achebe and his contemporaries battled as they attempted to resist the strain of their education which invariably privileged the work of the European masters. Additionally, Povey's testimony stresses the positive spirit of rivalry, the desire for fame, the sense of the charitable competition, which helped propel the creative frenzy among the group:

> In the early fifties at Ibadan University College a number of highly gifted young men attended class together. Their relationship seems to have touched off a spark that ignited each other's individual skills. Now the names, Wole Soyinka, J. P. Clark, Christopher Okigbo, along with Chinua Achebe, have become the most significant contemporary African writers . . . These writers have little in common with the efforts of Tutuola, for they are highly literate men, studied academically in English literature and as aware of current experimental trends in the poetry and drama in English as would be any young writer in this country [USA] . . . One can point to the influence of Ezra Pound on Okigbo and of Hopkins on Clark. One can demonstrate how Achebe draws upon the novels of Hardy and Soyinka upon the plays of Synge. These writers are eclectic as they develop their personal idioms. (1967: v)

It is necessary to quote this passage at length in order to establish as distinct a sense as one might of the enabling environment that was put in place for the constitution of the foundational literary texts of Nigerian nationalism, for the truth is that were it not for the level of cooperation they displayed with one another, merely bringing together talented persons of the calibre involved could have easily produced an explosive result of a different order. Were the aggregation to have led to the incitement of big egos among these young people, for instance, certainly a less positive outcome would have resulted. The key is that Achebe and his contemporaries inspired and positively challenged one another to do great things, instead of fighting among themselves for supremacy.

Thus, the fact that none of his contemporaries was moved by envy at the phenomenal success of Achebe's *Things Fall Apart* to produce a caustic parody to hold it up to public gaze and subject it to ridicule in, let us say, just such a manner as Henry Fielding's novel

Shamela (1740) is considered to be a hostile attack on Samuel Richardson's *Pamela* (1714), shows that the young Nigerians were rivals among whom there were strong bonds of affection. It is therefore a tribute to the goodwill they bore one another that in *Things Fall Apart* not only Achebe's immediate contemporaries but also their successors instantly detected a masterpiece and have returned to it over and over as their careers have progressed. In fact, as Bruce King (1993) has noted, comparable instances of extreme generosity were not to recur in Nigerian literary history. The supportive atmosphere that enabled each one of the founding fathers of modern Nigerian literature to attain a high level of success in their chosen crafts – Clark and Soyinka in drama, Okigbo in poetry, and Achebe in fiction – is a far cry from the cut-throat competitiveness that would bedevil the later generations.[4]

Critic M. J. C. Echeruo, who has singularly called attention to the period in which Achebe grew up as the most important element in the constitution of his personality, points to the fact that it was with Achebe's generation that 'the average Igbo boy of scant means was able to have university education and at home, too' (1975: 158). Growing up at a time like Achebe's, for Echeruo, bears other multiple implications – ideological, social, political and psychological:

> That generation brought into the life of the Igbo intellectual a kind of exhilarating and refreshing humour formed from a combination of past and present. It was this generation that chose or learnt to face life with both innocence and shrewdness, with a jovial but serious attitude which enabled it to face modernity without anger and without equivocation. Achebe's first roots have to be sought in that milieu. (1975: 158)

In the same essay, Echeruo warns that we risk underestimating the extraordinary genius that Achebe personally possesses if we overstress the role played by University College, Ibadan, in the development of his creativity. 'University College, Ibadan, inevitably became a venue where the brightest of the generation gathered for a four-year term of meditation; it also became the medium through which the idiom of the generation became that of the nation itself – a native idiom', Echeruo acknowledges (159). But, as he adds, 'Achebe belonged to a movement which University College, as an institution, did not initiate. If anything, it was by a technical accident that the University of Ibadan became the most important concentration of the best minds of the time reacting strongly and fervently against colonialism and finding fulfilment at that phase in the unity of African culture. It was in Achebe and his generation that the political agitations, the philosophical speculations, of the 1940s bore their first fruit, long before actual political independence in 1960' (159).

Echeruo is right on the mark; the primary sources of Achebe's writing are in the oral culture of his village, with which his missionary education that culminated at University College, Ibadan, along with the advent of print, came into collision. This tension is adequately reflected in his writing. His choice to stress the exciting new possibilities brought about by the peculiar circumstance of colonization owes something to his unique personal outlook: a serene, even-tempered personality, partly the result of growing up under the tutelage of parents who were sufficiently rooted in an African consciousness to develop the confidence to accept external Western influences as a part of their lives. This is a disposition an education under British missionary and colonial government control both reflected and reinforced. It is therefore only logical that the expanded opportunities for upward social mobility offered by Western education are among the unexpected positive aspects of colonization that Achebe emphasizes. With the work of a verbal magician like Achebe, the extraordinary result of the interplay of personal talent and a favourably disposed atmosphere is in its fullest display.

STUDY QUESTIONS

1. *Things Fall Apart* evidently is not a semi-autobiographical novel in the manner of *No Longer at Ease*, yet, at the same time, it reveals a great deal about Achebe's life in a similar way to how its Senegalese counterpart *God's Bits of Wood* (1960) discloses information about its author, Sembene Ousmane. In what ways can *Things Fall Apart* be viewed as a novel which is indirectly a reflection of Achebe's childhood experience? What aspects of Achebe's life story does one need to know in order to understand the novel?

2. A significant part of this chapter's argument is that an understanding of the history of European colonization permeates *Things Fall Apart*. What elements of the history of the encounter of the Igbos with the British do you think Achebe fully

grasped in the novel, and what aspects do you believe he did not? How do these matters add to or detract from the overall achievement of the novel?

3. How successful do you think Achebe in *Things Fall Apart* is in attempting to fulfil the role of the novelist he defines as being to lead 'the task of re-education and regeneration that must be done' (*Morning Yet on Creation Day*, 72)? Why should a writer in this context feel called upon to perform such a role? Do you think a novelist can meaningfully and effectively accomplish such a task without resorting to the ethnographic method? Do you consider such a project a gigantic gift or a burden?

CHAPTER 2

UNITY AND VARIETY IN STRUCTURE, LANGUAGE, STYLE AND FORM

A heavy reliance upon embedded narrative forms – anecdotes, animal fables, folktales, ballads, song-tales, parables, proverbs and myths – establishes Achebe's *Things Fall Apart* firmly as participating in the discourse of minimalist expression. The style of controlling excess is generally acknowledged as a major element of the short story. But, refusing to play by the rules of the game, Achebe in *Things Fall Apart* deftly grafts this method of extreme simplicity onto the more extended novelistic genre to capture the rich vibrancy and texture of a traditional Igbo culture in a memorable way. Throughout this novel, he uses an austere, spare, crisp, terse and highly suggestive Igbo-inflected English to great advantage. The infrastructural frame is evidently Western, modelled as *Things Fall Apart*'s plot is on the Aristotelian convention of tragedy, but the dominant rhetorical ploys used by Achebe are derived from oral tradition, one of the favourite indigenous arts of his people. Remarkably, *Things Fall Apart* does not merely carry traces of the oral storytelling performance situation; it replicates, evokes and simulates oral events in a raw form – not only through proverb rhetoric, contrary to the impression given by early commentators on the novel, important as proverb admittedly is to the novel's structure. Just as important to the story's rhetorical and narrative strategy are other Igbo-based idioms, thought patterns, beliefs and ritual practices.

THE POLITICS OF FOCALIZATION (NARRATIVE POINT OF VIEW)

There is, for sure, ample valid basis for *Things Fall Apart*'s acclaim as one of the undisputed masterpieces of world literature, although if it has any blemish at all it's a technical one having to do with the telling: the enigma of a story in which the narrator is not only a non-participant in the events narrated but is even unidentified. The lack of definiteness about the identity of the storyteller thus withholds from the text a requisite property of the historical novel, for, as has been noted long ago, 'by definition narrative art requires a story and a teller' and in 'the relationship between the teller and the tale, and that other relationship between the teller and the audience, lies the essence of narrative art' (Scholes and Kellogg, 1966: 240). The implication for the assessment of focalization (or what used to be called point of view in the discipline of narrative theory) of having a story with an unidentified narrator is grave: readers have difficulty determining who is manipulating events and actions. The elusive indeterminacy of the narrator's identity (in terms of age, background, gender, occupation, political affiliation, religion, social status or class, nationality, or other categorical distinctions) is a ground for misgivings because it has been confirmed that 'the first point almost anyone in the field of narrative will agree on nowadays with regard to narrators is that they should not be confused with authors. The narrator is variously described as an instrument, a construction, or a device wielded by the author' (Abbott, 2002: 63).[1]

Mainly because deployment of an instrument, a construction, or a device is always both purposeful and affective, when a story gets told without having an identifiable narrator, especially a story about events believed to be historical facts as *Things Fall Apart* is, it is logical that readers will become curious about whose story it is, about who the teller is. In a nutshell, since the identity of the narrator is inseparable from focalization, the mode by means of which a story's actions, characters, events, dialogue, setting and mood are presented, the construction of the fictive persons is one of those areas about which questions could be raised, none more seriously in *Things Fall Apart* than that of the personality assigned the protagonist, hero Okonkwo: how it is he is known and projected as a remnant brute, a savage in a surprisingly thoroughly civilized setting; a character plagued by a need for more sensitivity, chiefly among his society's acknowledged, well laid-down and constantly regulated rules of conduct for gentlemen.

Anyone who has the presence of mind to look closely would see that Okonkwo's lack of self-composure indicates that something isn't right as his bearing is clearly out of line. The mark of excess and license typifying extreme ambition, the attributes of Okonkwo are so egregiously in conflict with his background that they both call attention to themselves and work against his characterization, calling into question the motive of his construction. How can a society with interwoven evidence of self-regulated balance so impossible to deny produce a man so decidedly at odds with its own values, a monster so terribly awkward about the way he acts? Why does Achebe make undoubtedly his first anti-imperial campaigner a beast, a man completely without brains? Of whose imaginative projection is he? Why is he so different from the rest of the Igbo men presented in the novel? For example, why doesn't Okonkwo have anything in common with either his own father Unoka or his own son Nwoye?

Are the contrasting personalities of his best friend Obierika, and Obierika's own son Maduka, as well as of Okonkwo's own uncle Uchendu, and those of Ezeudu, the oldest man in his region, so outlined because the demands of the plot require them to be that way just to keep the narrative going? About the means by which Okonkwo is figured out, readers are certainly entitled to want to know more. It would be interesting to know, for example, if Okonkwo is based on an actual historical figure, as Charles Nnolim indicates that the figure of Ezeulu is in *Arrow of God* (1977: 2). From whose point of view is Okonkwo seen and projected? Who is the mask behind the mask, the all-hearing, all-seeing, all-knowing observer and commentator in *Things Fall Apart*? Through whose eyes do readers come to view people, events, experiences, in this novel?[2]

Okonkwo acts as though he believes he is within the bounds of the values and codes of his society. Since he is not seen to be insisting on a course of action which people believe he knows to be wrong, that speaks well for his sincerity of purpose. He may lack a contemplative understanding of his actions, but once set in his ways Okonkwo's attitude hardens and gravitates in a direction that everyone knows is wrong-headed. He is rendered as someone both alienated from his society's codes of conduct and deeply involved in its mainstream social life; both an adjudicator or custodian of the law and a headstrong outlaw. Through whose eyes are readers given access into Okonkwo's make up? Of whose vision of the Igbo's personality is Okonkwo's image a projection? These questions cry out to be settled by careful reading and analysis. Giving Okonkwo the mysterious stature of being a remote, larger-than-life figure, yet a social and political leader of a community whose core values he defies does indicate that he is a caricature, but this in turn raises the question about the place of caricatures in historical reconstruction. The full implications of Okonkwo's depiction are particularly revealed when consideration is given to Dorrit Cohn's argument that 'historical works, journalistic reports, biographies, and autobiographies, are subject to judgments of truth and falsity' (1999: 15). Within such a formulation, veracity or the degree of faithfulness to historical fact ought to rank just as high on the scale as the novel's representation of culture is usually taken to be in *Things Fall Apart*'s interpretation. In the absence of a clearly identified narrator, what readers have a right to demand to know is from whose state of mind or perspective people, events, actions and places in the novel are constructed; who is the mediating intelligence of the story.

Questions about the identity of *Things Fall Apart*'s teller seem important because they intersect with those relating to the text's representational assumptions, how far the text's presentation of experience can be accepted. To broach this subject of representation is to raise questions of motive since authorship invariably comes with the unavoidable burden of textual ownership. Like any author, Achebe cannot be exculpated from responsibility for his text. This is the sense in which the way *Things Fall Apart* has been constructed can be taken as a mirror of some of the ways in which the educated colonial subject is predisposed, even while disparaging or condemning the unjust practices of colonial rule, to play the conniving role of adopting and perpetuating popular native stereotypes that have existed in the West. As Gayatri Spivak reminds us, this is a role commonly associated with the 'native informant' (1999: 4).[3]

The subject matter of *Things Fall Apart*'s informing vision is thus clearly not one to be taken lightly, even granted that in as much as language is often a vehicle of culture, a distinction can occasionally be made between indoctrination on one hand and foreign language acquisition and adoption on the other. As a literature that has emerged out of the cultural hybrid formed by the collision between Europe and Africa, *Things Fall Apart* is an instance where the lines between indoctrination and language adoption are partly blurred. That is why Abiola Irele should be taken seriously when he urges the reader not to be taken in by appearance, since 'as a modern novelist, Achebe is hardly in the same position as a traditional storyteller, creating his stories unselfconsciously out of the full sense of coincidence with the culture within which he practices his art and that provides objective support for his imaginative projections' (2001: 119).

Having said that, it needs as well to be recognized that one of the paradoxes of colonization is how rather than leading to a complete divorce or sterility, the encounter has led to artistic fusion and a generous flowering of letters. Politically, bringing Africa and Europe together created difficult companions. But the books that have come out of the marriage, like Achebe's *Things Fall Apart*, bear the marks of a variegated gallery of art with remarkable vitality which can be imagined to be the product of only one kind of experience: the unique chemistry of conditions of unresolved contradictions to which colonization gave vent. Partly because Igbo forms of vernacular rhetoric tend to blend themselves easily with English expression, they allow for full-scale fictional exploration in *Things Fall Apart*, leading to a new form of language that enables Achebe to present Africa to the world through mediated lenses. That is why it's not entirely correct to conclude that Achebe's 'newly acquired tongue' necessarily places his ideas at 'a considerable structural and expressive remove from the speech modes, habits of thought, and cultural codes of the historical community whose experience he undertakes to record in his fiction' (Irele, 2001: 119).[4] On the contrary, as a literature of cultural hybridization, the hallmarks of *Things Fall Apart*'s accomplishments lie in conveying an amazing story with great aesthetic effect, exemplifying in so doing a supreme instance of successful pastiche.

THE SEDUCTIONS OF SPEECH: TRANSLATION, IGBO THOUGHTS, ENGLISH MEDIUM OF EXPRESSION

Once readers get past the technical matter of the telling, they should encounter in *Things Fall Apart* a highly engrossing text. Achebe not only has a superb command of English, but he also possesses rare and unmatched skills for marshalling and subjecting the minutest details of experience into ordered patterns, and in *Things Fall Apart* the writing is supple, fresh and compelling. English and Igbo thought patterns fuse harmoniously. As good an example as any of this linguistic harmony is Ekwefi's reprimanding comments to her daughter Ezinma while the two help in getting the food ready for the bride-pricing reception of Akueke, Obierika's daughter:

'Remove your *jigida* first,' her mother warned as she moved near the fireplace to bring the pestle resting against the wall. 'Every day I tell you that *jigida* and fire are not friends. But you will never hear. You grew ears for decoration, not for hearing. One of these days your *jigida* will catch fire on your waist, and then you will know.' (50)[5]

This passage summons to life not only the rhythm, rhetoric and verbal echo, but also the light, gentle tenor of Igbo speech, which, rendered into English, gives the remarks they carry a new vigour. A conventional English way of communicating the same thoughts might be for Ekwefi to tell Ezinma not to have on her flammable beads while cooking and give a stern warning about the high price she fears her daughter might sooner than later pay for repeatedly ignoring sound advice. But such a construction would not just exhibit bland, unresourceful phrasing, it would zap the sting of humour or verbal delight and liveliness out of the reproving remarks.

But, as phrased, the ideas are more forcefully conveyed in something akin to the language of poetry. Only one Igbo word, *jigida* (beads), occurs in the speech; yet it creates a heightening effect in a speech characterized by a highly figurative, metaphorical, Igbo-inflected construction. Giving Ekwefi's speech its special liveliness is the way she personifies '*jigida* and fire' as arch-enemies. In addition, to emphasize how aberrational stubbornness is, in reprimanding her obstinate daughter for not heeding useful advice ('But you will never hear'), Ekwefi characterizes her as someone who 'grew' her 'ears for decoration, not for hearing'. Of course by saying Ezinma 'will never hear', Ekwefi doesn't mean that the words never reach her daughter's eardrums, but that she refuses to get the words into her spirit. The phenomenon of ears that are mere protuberances (i.e. ears resisting being put to normal use as they should) therefore not only presents a powerful visual image to capture the aberrant behaviour of a girl who refuses to follow parental instruction, but it also paints a picture of a great monstrosity – a girl who stands out because of her deformed ugly face. Since this is a culture where possession of beauty or the perfect female body is a girl's most important asset, and where employing witty jokes in the gentle instruction of young girls is a common maternal responsibility, helping Ezinma to see the stupidity and ugliness of her attitude by making her laugh is not only in line with responsible satirization but an effective use of shock therapy to cure misguided behaviour.

Describing the enigmatic effects of living and working under a second-language situation imposed by colonization, Nigerian feminist critic and poet Molara Ogundipe-Leslie makes an observation which is extremely relevant for understanding *Things Fall Apart*:

> Why do some of us write in English which is not our mother-tongue? And what is the experience of writing in English, especially for a poet? We gained a facility with English and achieved a proficiency well beyond that in our mother-tongues, due to the colonial experience. The proficiency varies from person to person. Some are able still to speak their mother-tongue better while they remain fluent in written English; others have their fluency in both the writing and the speaking of mother-tongue permanently interfered with by the colonial experience. Still others end up not being able to speak the mother-tongue at all. (1995: 103)

Like the African poets who write in European languages, Achebe obviously did not adopt English by choice but as a matter of necessity defined by colonial rule. Nevertheless, by giving his writing international currency, English has turned out to be more an enabling than an inhibiting factor for him. Caught between his mother-tongue and an English language imposed by colonial education, the result of this union is codified in the special variety of English language in which *Things Fall Apart* is expressed. This is an English language that has been adjusted to serve as a vehicle for conveying the potency of Igbo idioms, turns of phrase, concepts, ideas and words.[6]

Many tacitly assume that, to meet the demand to express Igbo concepts and ideas accurately, Achebe had to reconfigure in a second-language situation the tenor of his native idiom. However, until recently, readers of African literature have been more accustomed to reading about claims of how Achebe's powers of persuasion were derived from the utilization of his Igbo ethnic group's art of storytelling than seeing demonstrations of that reality.[7] It's thanks to a surge of interest in the structures of African narratives over the past decade or so that we are now better informed. Chantal Zabus, for example, provides a telling broad outline of the models from which modern African writers generally draw when she refers to their penchant for expropriating 'discursive elements ranging from rules of address, riddles, praise-names and dirges to the use of proverbs' as resources that 'constitute the ethno-text which is grafted onto the European-language narrative, in an attempt to recapture traditional speech and atmosphere' (1991: 133). More specifically, regarding techniques made famous in Achebe's fiction, Zabus's observation that 'proverbs, maxims, apophthegms and epigrams are the main discursive elements which the author lifts from orature to recapture traditional speech and atmosphere' (1991: 136) is important and needs further elaboration because *Things Fall Apart* has an ethno-linguistic consciousness that has never quite been exhaustively defined.

The elements described by Chantal Zabus should therefore be considered along with those earlier mentioned in the opening paragraph of this chapter: anecdotes, animal fables, folktales, ballads, song-tales and myths. As Emmanuel Obiechina, a scholar who has brought long-needed attention to an aspect of these techniques – that of the miniature story – shows in a seminal essay, not only does Achebe's fiction betray a lingering affiliation to Igbo storytelling tradition, but the oral echoes in his novels are also a signal that the laments about the demise of storytelling in the wake of writing are largely exaggerated (1993). It is one of the excitements of our times that traditional storytelling not only continues to thrive in the village settings; but we can also savour its vibrant afterlife in the works of African novelists, who graft its forms onto their fiction. In particular, Obiechina's discussion of what he calls 'the story-within-the-story or the narrative proverb' (1993: 124), another name for anecdotes, animal fables, ballads, folktales, song-tales and myths that are used to advance or reiterate the central idea of the bigger story in African fiction, is definitive and I cannot see it ever being surpassed.

While acknowledging in the essay that there is a pervasive use of 'narrative embedding' in African fiction, Obiechina presents *Things Fall Apart* as 'the best example of the use of narrative proverbs to express the distinctive quality of the African fiction'. For Obiechina, Achebe's novel stands out clearly as 'the most elaborate and the most successful use of this technique for diverse formal, thematic, and aesthetic purposes' (1993: 127). Obiechina then proceeds to look at nine embedded narratives, 'of which seven are folktales and mythic stories, one a pseudo-history, and one an anecdote', showing how each 'brings something to the total meaning of the novel, some insight to clarify the action, to sharpen characterization, to elaborate themes and enrich the setting and environment of action'. 'Most importantly', he argues, 'the narrative proverbs help to define the epistemological order within the novel' (1993: 127).

These stories include the 'cosmic myth of the quarrel between Earth and sky', one of the favourite tales told to Nwoye by his mother against his father Okonkwo's wishes that the young man delight more in 'masculine stories of violence and bloodshed' (Achebe, 1958: 37–8); 'the Locust Myth and Ikemefuna's song' (38–9, 42), both of which immediately precede Ikemefuna's execution in his third year as a hostage in Okonkwo's household and anticipate as well as comment on it. The others are 'the Mosquito Myth' (42), narrated soon after Ikemefuna's murder to highlight the intractability of a problem that would not go away; the story of 'the Tortoise and the Birds' (67–70), told to Ezinma by her mother Ekwefi to teach a lesson about greed and self-centredness; 'The Abame Story' (97), conveying news of the first Igbo village to be wiped out by European colonists and relayed to Okonkwo during his exile in Mbanta by his friend Obireka to warn against unprovoked assault; 'The Kite Myth' (98–9), recounted by Okonkwo's uncle Uchendu to explain why events like Abame's destruction are preventable; the tale of 'the Snake-Lizard Myth' (59), incoherently related by Ezinma to buttress the values Igbo attach to hard work and professionalism; and then the story of the 'Thieves of Umuike' (79), told mainly for comical effect by Obierika to distantiate the people of Umofia from their strange, dishonest neighbours who use powerful medicine to steal.

Add to the detailed list provided by Obiechina the tale of Obiako, the palm-wine tapster who would not respond positively to the Oracle's request that he offer a goat as a sacrifice to his dead father to forestall falling off a palm tree to his death. Since Obiako's action is based on his reasoning that his dead father is undeserving of a sacrificial goat since he never even 'had a fowl when he was alive' (15), his story reminds us strongly of Okonkwo's. From the formal standpoint, all the stories work in tandem with proverbs proper to help keep the novel's plot glued together despite its episodic narrative frame. Though the main plot falls into three main movements – the first devoted to life in Umofia and hero Okonkwo's career before his exile in Mbanta; the second devoted to life during his exile; and the third devoted to life after his return from exile to a drastically changed Umofia under colonial control – the work has much coherence largely because the sequence of events is logically connected, and the conflicts are rigorously worked out, as every part is made to contribute to the overall movement of the story. Despite the fractured plot that is brought about by the way Okonkwo's exile in Mbanta appears to freeze narrative time, an exquisitely crafted language blending a colourful native idiom and animated proverbial usage, animal fable, and myths enables *Things Fall Apart* to establish both cohesiveness and particularities of place and of expression.

It is a striking feature of this novel, then, that the plan to employ specificity of context to render a balance between the often competing aims of persuasive general statement and accurate representation has been well served by the text's allegorical framework. As noted by Obiechina, the embedded stories collaborate with proverbs proper to confer upon *Things Fall Apart*'s overarching narrative frame 'two main principles of the African oral tradition': 'authority and association – by which an idea is given validity by being placed side by side with another idea that bears the stamp of communal approval and by its being linked to the store-house of collective wisdom' and 'an illustrative, authoritative support to an idea, a point of view, a perception, or perspective in conversation or oral discourse' which is thus 'vested with much greater significance than is the case in the non-traditional context' (1993: 125). There is no doubt that all the embedded narratives are 'organically integrated to the development of form and content of *Things Fall Apart*' (Obiechina, 1993: 138).

PROVERBS AS EXPRESSIONS OF IGBO AESTHETICS, BELIEFS, CUSTOMS, IDEAS

As many have noticed, it seems fairly obvious that proverbs are central to the art of speaking among the Igbo. Reflecting this reality of the Igbo love of rhetorical display, like Achebe's other novels, *Things Fall Apart* employs this piquant style of expression not only to convey the values and wisdom of the Igbos but also to add colour and spice to their speech. Achebe himself refers to their power when he describes proverbs in an often quoted phrase in the novel as 'the palm oil with which words are eaten' (1958: 5). The proverb is, he elaborates more fully elsewhere in an interview with Kalu Ogbaa, 'both a functional means of communication and also a very elegant

and artistic performance itself. I think that proverbs are both utilitarian and little vignettes of art. So when I use these forms in my
novels, they both serve a utilitarian purpose, which is to re-enact the
life of the people that I am describing and also delight through elegance and aptness of imagery. This is what proverbs are supposed to
do' (1981: 5).

Now, it may be said that all literary forms are as much concerned
with what they say as with how they say it. There is no doubt that
the distinguishing quality of literature is its acute self-consciousness
about its being. However, by their very exacting nature, proverbs
bear the marks of an even greater rhetorical self-consciousness. As
one of the emblems of succinct expression, proverbs manifest an
overwhelming urge for perfection in phraseology. It is not surprising
that, though they might appear to be mere decorative or embroi-
dered speech acts, proverbs seldom fail to possess quintessential linguistic vitality that additionally embodies the wisdom of the ages
gleaned from the routine experiences of a people. It is therefore not
just that proverbs are infrequent in Achebe's novels – hardly any
such really innovative elements of style are ever in over-abundant
supply – but that they are employed mostly by elders considered to
be the custodians of culture. For the most part, the few that exist are
used to give counsel almost always at key narrative moments and
they are therefore, with good reason, activated quite sparingly in
Things Fall Apart (where only a total of 23 or so of them are featured, in contrast, for example, with a minimum of 139 found in
Arrow of God).

Even bearing in mind, as Kwesi Yankah has noticed too from his
meticulous study of the speech habits of the Akan people of Ghana,
that 'the form and meaning of the proverb are not fixed' (1989: 28),
what is surprising in this regard is not that studies of proverbs in
Achebe's fiction proliferate, but that proverbs in Achebe's novels are
so susceptible to being misinterpreted or conflated with other unrelated figures of speech – for example, axioms, metaphors and similes
– even by native Igbo scholars. For instance, Emmanuel Egar is not
completely accurate in giving his tortuous interpretation of the
proverb, 'A chick that will grow into a cock can be spotted the very
day it hatches' (46).

'In this short piece', Egar claims, 'Achebe knowingly gives one
strand of meaning to cause and effect . . . a chick will grow into a
cock, which is a simple enunciation of cause and effect. But is this

true? Is it not possible that a chick may not grow into a cock if the environment is too harsh and not conducive to growth? A chick might be eaten by snakes and wild animals. It could die by accident' (2000: xiii). Endlessly pursuing a hypothetical debate makes Egar totally miss the real point of the proverb, which is about Okonkwo's psychological burden – his grave anxieties concerning issues of succession. But the fear Okonkwo has is that his eyes cannot possibly betray him. Nwoye is not holding up much promise as a son because all signs are pointing to one fact: Nwoye is disappointingly not acting like he can become the man he should be. Okonkwo cannot be deceived about this matter of grave import because action speaks louder than words. The idea that the character of a person may somehow be decoded through his or her actions thus suggests behaviour as the only reliable ground of reference and truth, enabling Okonkwo's thoughts to draw their effect from analogy with a reading of the behaviour of birds, among whom the fact that appearances cannot deceive for long is an undisputable reality.

The rhetoric of proverb, of the illustrative action, is a rhetoric that requires a shift of focus from situation or surrounding to the defining qualities of the exemplifying act, from the context in which the phenomenon occurs to the narrated conduct itself. That is why a reader obsessed with situation or context attacks the authority on which proverb logic is located. No wonder Egar's rendition not only misconstrues the premise upon which proverbs base their truth claims – the fact that both the speaker of proverbs and the addressee assume a controlled condition as an *a priori* or a given point of reference. That might also explain why Egar woefully misses the sexually suggestive joke played by the chick caught in the unbecoming and premature – even if innocent – misconduct of mounting the back of its own mother, an act that is an obvious simulation of the future sexual act it will perform as a cock on heat. An audience that will experience the full force of the line must have both a sharp wit and mental agility. Such an audience will know that behaviour is the most reliable revelation of true nature and real character, and the world of birds confirms this even with what is apparently innocent conduct. Since proverbs derive their meaning from keen observation of manners – the character cues they leave – a too contextually obsessed approach, like Egar's, can become so reductive as to easily lead to their misinterpretation.

Clearly what the study of proverbs in Achebe's novels now lacks and sorely requires is both a contextual and an integrative analysis. The proverb about the mischief of the chick should therefore be considered along with the preceding one, with which it forms a link, 'Where are the young suckers that will grow when the old banana tree dies?' (46), which is the framework for the question raised by Okonkwo for Obierika's contemplation, as part of a key rhetorical argument during their conversation. That discussion, centred on the two men's separate families' futures, is appropriately conducted on the occasion of the wedding of Obierika's son, Maduka, a good moment for Okonkwo to begin thinking seriously aloud about his own son's coming of age. Both proverbs thus form a network with another: 'As our fathers said, you can tell a ripe corn by its looks' (16). All three of them collaborate in helping to relay Okonkwo's exasperations over Nwoye's lack of drive, Okonkwo's fears that he lacks an industrious son to hand things over to. The ground for his worries is glaringly obvious because identity cannot be hidden.

Obierika attempts to reassure his friend that it's too early to give up all hope, 'The children are still very young' (46). But both men know that Obierika's is just a polite manner of speaking, a vacuous form of encouragement. As cogently relayed in another proverb, justifying Okonkwo's fears is the fact that 'when mother-cow is chewing grass its young ones watch its mouth' (49). That expression is Okonkwo's way of conclusively stating that his son Nwoye's non-acceptance of his father's leadership is what makes his case a hopeless one. Nwoye's refusal to submit under the influence of his father has deprived him of the guidance and nourishment every child needs to ease the pains of growing up. Now, this doesn't mean, of course, that Nwoye cannot develop through self-reliance, but only that the absence of schooling or apprenticeship must be seen as a major self-imposed handicap or denial to oneself of culture, difficult for a boy to try to overcome on his own on the slippery road to becoming a man. Okonkwo should know about the hurdle a young person should expect to overcome when trying to face the pressure of adversity alone because his own career is a powerful example of it.

It would appear that the special treasure of receiving instruction under the tutelage of one's parent will be all too evident, but the Igbos have a proverb to explain and define more clearly the concept: 'A child's fingers are not scalded by a piece of hot yam which its mother puts into its palm' (47). Okonkwo cites this proverb to rationalize his carrying out the Oracle's wishes by participating in

Ikemefuna's execution because it puts forward a belief of the Igbos that parental instruction is always in the service of what is considered appropriate and consistent with the child's best interest. For the Igbo, it is unreasonable to expect a parent to ask his or her child to do something which will harm the child. Igbo custom requires all parents to know better than to carry out parental teaching, reproof, correction and training outside of the child's welfare.

Among the variety of purposes that proverbs serve in *Things Fall Apart*, an important one is for character portrayal or revelation of states of mind. 'As the Ibo say: When the moon is shining the cripple becomes hungry for a walk' (7) is a striking one quoted to reflect the agitated state of Okonkwo's mind while lying in bed the night before Umofia takes the decision to carry out the duty of revenge for Mbaino's murder of a daughter of Umofia. He hears strong war drum sounds summoning Umofia into preparedness for battle, and they trigger his fond memories of the greatest joys he has ever known as a warrior. Here, language takes the form of drum sounds bringing back to life, in a flood, an onrush of emotion that has been buried within Okonkwo. What is significant is the proverb's exposure of the way symbolic action like war drum sounds can stir up a warrior's charging spirits that have been suppressed for a long time by prolonged absence of warfare. The proverb encapsulates the power of coded message, the deep effect the language of drums can have in re-igniting the old flames of warriordom, the rising voracious appetite for heroic action within Okonkwo, the fury for bloodletting carnage that had been held in during the lull caused by the cessation of hostilities. By this proverb, the novel is intent upon sustaining Okonkwo's personality, his warmongering instinct, which later becomes somewhat dormant, and then suddenly rises again when he cuts down Ikemefuna, his foster child. It is the same emotion that spurs him on to murder the Court Messenger and then terminally to accomplish his own self-annihilation to bring a closure to his towering career in violence toward the end of the novel. The appropriateness of the proverb lies in the way it is quoted to capture a state of mind in which Okonkwo's emotion is under very great pressure, as he has been stressed to breaking point.

When true to its form, a successful proverb therefore represents an amazing use of dialect to convey wisdom based on understanding of the observed natural world of the speaker as well as the cultural habits of the group as a whole. The very first one in *Things Fall*

Apart, 'He who brings kola brings life' (5), exhibits this property of the proverb as an absorbing utterance, its ability to succinctly express a social outlook. Used by credit grantor Okoye during a visit to collect a debt from Unoka, hero Okonkwo's father, this particular one is a gracious way for the debt collector to say that he is committed to not violating the rule of hospitality extended to him because he understands protocol, the concord demanded by the formality of the occasion. And so, upon hearing this, the audience as well as readers of the novel here encounter the visitor conveying assurances to his host that the cordiality extended to him will be reciprocated during the tense moments usually expected to accompany the difficult deliberations involved in debt repayment negotiations, of which the one of Okoye's visit is a typical example.

Thus, in return, Unoka responds in the same spirit by quoting another proverb shortly after the exchange of niceties, when they settle down to business and Okoye verbalizes the purpose of his visit as being to exact repayment of the debt he is owed: 'Our elders say that the sun shines on those who stand before it shines on those who kneel under them. I shall pay my first debts first' (6). By this, Unoka is using the authority of tradition to convey a self-defensive statement that he is not delaying repaying the debt without a purpose but is following a schedule of debt repayment dictated by common logic, namely that of chronology, sanctioned by the group, the belief that acquittance of debt will follow a law of nature, as implicitly a fair and therefore better schedule than any arbitrary one like repaying the creditor who called first.

Speaking in the same vocabulary with his creditor gives special resonance to Unoka's appeal to their shared claim to traditional justice and truth. Its effectiveness lies not only in the way the proverb aids in momentarily easing out the friction that could potentially have been provoked with a more abrasive form of verbal exchange. More importantly, the potency of the speech act lies in how it successfully negotiates a debt repayment truce for Unoka. In what looks like an arrangement that obviously has achieved a little more than is expected, Unoka's important accomplishment is graced further by his not simply getting Okoye in line but putting him in a light-hearted or humorous frame of mind while he returns home to wait patiently.

In addition to helping Unoka to put his case to his creditor, the speech betrays his proclivity for grace, humour and wit, all of which underscore a broad contrast between his personality and that of his son, Okonkwo. Unoka is considered lazy and improvident but he is an articulate and deft negotiator. On the other hand, he happens to have a son who is enterprising but brusque and inarticulate. This style of communication thus contributes powerfully toward foreshadowing a key theme in the novel: the contrast between the dialogical and confrontational personalities and the implications they bear for conflict resolution. Through the gifts of elocution, Unoka, who is scorned, talks his way out of difficult situations with remarkable poise. But his more enterprising son is lacking even in those modest skills, leaving readers to wonder what would happen if, rather than putting his hands too quickly to work to cut down the Court Messenger, Okonkwo would instead see fit to open up a conversation with him. His suicide might be averted; we would of course have a different novel, which might not necessarily replicate the impact of *Things Fall Apart* as we have it, but he would certainly have helped change the novel's narrated course of history.

One of the baffling tragic ironies of colonization is that the traditional wisdom which seemed to serve Africans well in helping them to negotiate and balance the complexities of social and political relations in their world did not adequately equip them to defend themselves in the context of a European presence. The experience of the Igbos did not differ in this respect from that common experience of Africans, because colonialism introduced entirely different codes of conduct which not only came into sharp conflict with, but caused major modifications to, the truth claims of their core values.

Key tenets of the Igbo belief system particularly come under attack, including Igbo notions of generosity, duality, reciprocity, humility and tolerance, whose mindset finds its way into the proverbial lore of the group. 'As the elders said, if a child washed his hands he could eat with kings' (6) is quoted, for example, to remind Okonkwo of the Igbo democratic spirit to which he owes his social mobility and without which none of his aspirations to rise up the social ladder would have amounted to much: the practice of determining social status not exclusively by hereditary aristocracy and monarchy but also through individual effort due to Igbo recognition of the constitutive duality of existence.

It is clear that the ideal of proper manners is invoked in anticipation of the reproof Okonkwo's excessive snobbery toward those less successful than himself will later incur, a reproach embodied in two other related proverbs ('Looking at a king's mouth . . . one would think he never sucked at his mother's breast'; 'those whose palm-kernels are cracked for them by a benevolent spirit should not forget to be humble' [19]). It is also evident that the Igbos recognize that it is foolish to despise the days of small beginnings because of their dialectical world-view, a belief in the contraries of life expressed in the saying 'when a man says *yes* his *chi* says *yes* also', which acknowledges that success is unattainable without personal effort (hence Okonkwo 'said *yes* very strongly; so his *chi* agreed. Not only his *chi* but his clan too, because it judged a man by the work of his hand' [19]). All of that notwithstanding, a deeply moving irony of the situation created by colonialism, with which *Things Fall Apart* deals, is that when values like duality, tolerance, humility and gene-rosity, which provided the conditions for growth in traditional Igbo society, become transposed into the colonial context, the conse-quences are deadly.

Thus, the idea embodied in the proverbs 'You will have what is good for you and I will have what is good for me. Let the kite perch and let the eagle perch too. If one says no to the other, let its wings break' and 'I have brought you this little kola. As our people say, a man who pays respect to the great paves the way for his own great-ness' (14) becomes problematic within the context of colonization. The idea conveyed in those sayings, as quoted by Okonkwo to place his request for Nwakibie to lend him some seed yams, issues from the wisdom enshrined in the adage that 'one good turn deserves another'. It in turn clearly sketches the commonly shared belief of the Igbos that there is always room enough for everyone in every circumstance. The same concept is rephrased in another proverb: 'as the dog said, "If I fall down for you and you fall down for me, it's play"' (51) is quoted to ease the haggling tussle at Obierika's daugh-ter Akueke's bride-pricing event. But the paradox is that the same values necessary for sustaining a community – the belief that one good turn deserves another, the notions of duality, reciprocity, accommodation, and acceptance of others – can also be responsible for its collapse. Essentially this is the reality seen with special direct-ness when the Christian missionaries arrive in Mbanta.

The missionaries request a piece of land to settle on, and the elders of the clan oblige by giving them the evil forest. The elders act in part because they believe the evil forest is 'alive with sinister forces and powers of darkness' (105). But their action is also consis-tent with the Igbo ethic of tolerance which predisposes them to accommodate the contraries of life, the idea that where one thing stands another also stands beside it. However, during the times of rapid change, the values of the European settlers prove themselves the diametrical opposite of such practices. Hence, this generosity not only renders the Igbo community susceptible to European penetration, but it actually facilitates the European conquest resoundingly. Once established, Christians initiate a rapid evangelization of Igboland, beginning with the persuasive use of songs to convert marginalized groups like the *osus*, the non-titled and rejected.

It is not surprising that, not long afterwards, conversion turns violent. The extremist evangelist Reverend Smith takes over from the liberal Reverend Brown, an apostle of peaceable conversion and co-existence, and replaces Mr Kiaga, Brown's assistant, with radical convert Enoch. Reverend Smith's militant message encourages Enoch to commit the grave offenses of disrobing an *egwugwu* and killing a royal python. The revolutionary Christian leaders then turn loose on the general populace. Henceforth, attitudes displayed by the Christians don't give the impression that they believe anyone else worthy to exist. Following their forward-looking nature, the Igbos prize progress, newness and individual achievement, and are therefore habituated to adapting to changing circumstances, as testified by the proverb 'Eneke the bird says that since men have learnt to shoot without missing, he has learnt to fly without perching' (16). The evidence for Igbo adaptability to change is even more strongly asserted in another proverb: 'A toad does not run in the day time for nothing' (20). Quoted to explain the puzzling story of Obiako, a palm-wine tapper who unexpectedly gives up his trade, it points to the fact that there is always a dramatic reason behind every major event. Nevertheless, despite their well-attuned disposition to behaviour modification, the new exclusivity introduced by Christianity poses challenges that catch the Igbos unawares; off guard, as it were. That explains the massive scale of discomfiture caused by the European impact.

But by no means should we underestimate proverbs' usefulness, especially as a self-authenticating tool in the concern with self-defence. This is particularly true when a trying situation calls for a need for an individual to overturn a negative image of him- or herself. 'The lizard that jumped from the high iroko tree to the ground said he would praise himself if no one else did' (15–16) is quoted; for instance, by Okonkwo as a part of the argument he is putting forward to persuade Nwakibie to lend him seed yams. By this proverb, Okonkwo is saying that credit is fully deserved: he can be relied upon to pay back; trust is in order; his portfolio should speak for itself; the collateral represented by his personal record of achievement is creditworthy. Outstanding performance should bring respect and his monumental accomplishments should not go under-appreciated. This proverb implies that, when working in a hostile environment, a little expression of one's sense of self-importance (some call it boastfulness) is good medicine for the soul, for in a setting where image is everything, and where one does not have an audience ready and waiting to applaud one's achievements, there, one should grant oneself self-congratulation. A little critique of representation is in order because one needs to participate in the work of representation by displacing representations of one by others.

The saying thus harks back obliquely to the major theme of the novel, *Things Fall Apart*'s very reason for being, and unquestionably also Achebe's own professed writing manifesto, as elaborated in the essay 'The Novelist as Teacher' (1965, reprinted 1975), in which he says his goal as an author is to help his society to regain its belief in itself after the depredations of colonial rule. If there is one strict principle at stake in this philosophical outlook, it is the underlying idea that resources are released to those who are at peace with themselves, to those who have a comfortable conception of themselves, for it does not matter what the opinions of others about one are because the key for success is inner consonance; the source of one's greatest enemy is not external but inner dissonance.

Indeed, the ethical status of one's obligatory duty to remain in an ever self-renewing, self-defencive mood is re-established beyond dispute in at least one other proverb: 'as the saying goes, an old woman is always uneasy when dry bones are mentioned in a proverb' (15). This proverb is quoted to capture Okonkwo's unease during the narration of the story of the blatant disrespect shown to his own father by palm-wine tapster Obiako based on his sense that his father did not leave his children a worthy legacy. However, despite the spiteful garrulousness and insensitivity of those seeking to embarrass Okonkwo with a reality that strikes too close to home for him, one could argue that the fundamental subject of the proverb is not so much or not only the shame and humiliation provoked by a public display of an invasive reality one has no wish to be associated with. There is cause for irritation in hearing derogatory remarks about oneself or about being held in contempt or ridiculed in an honour-based culture such as that of the Igbos, but it is humiliation that prompts one to aspire to social distinction and rank.

For that reason, social discomfort becomes a metaphor for situations out of which responsibility arises. By the time he wrote *Things Fall Apart*, therefore, Achebe was an incurable optimist to have put forward the claim that the Igbos discover in the insults of colonization a ready-made situation for self-examination, the primary key to self-knowledge. If there is a single ideological element which makes Achebe a charismatic personality, one of the most universally beloved writers, that element is most assuredly his restraint, a disposition to ease out tensions through non-violent means, the unconscious spirit governing the composition of all but his latest novel, *Anthills of the Savannah*. Where more combative writers would call for a bloody struggle against white supremacy, Achebe uses Okonkwo's blundering extremism and pathetic defeat in *Things Fall Apart* instead to campaign about (or at the very least hint at or suggest) the undesirability (or even futility) of such a course of action. Essentially the story of a self-assured society and its fall under the throes of foreign intrusion, a traditional society's unsuccessful attempt to rise out of the ashes of a colossal assault it encounters on its own turf gives Achebe a reason to assign a greater role to language than military violence in that journey toward recovery. Because it abounds in narrative genres that both charm with their eloquence the unsophisticated reader and prove themselves worth reading and pondering to the sophisticated, what Monica Furlong claims for John Bunyan's *Pilgrim's Progress* can be justifiably claimed for *Things Fall Apart*: that in the masterpiece we encounter 'the marks of a work of genius: imaginative vitality, astounding originality and touches of sublimity' (1997: vii). With the publication of *Things Fall Apart*, Achebe made a signal contribution to the development of African English-language fiction. He fundamentally altered the range of English expression by tapping from Igbo thought patterns and idioms, injecting a new energy into the English expressive mode, and conferring on the Igbo base language and ideas of the world an international currency, while deploying them in contexts which still enable the materials to retain their local resonance.

SUGGESTIONS FOR FURTHER STUDY

1. Each segment of Achebe's deceptively simple story repays close attention to detail. In order to throw light on this text as a variously variegated and ornamented work of art, focus should be on the interplay between speech acts and novelistic procedure. Consider, for example, the importance of songs and hymns; the function of contrastive characterization, Okonkwo pitched against Obierika, Unoka against Okoye; the aesthetic position suggested by anecdotal device; how appropriately the opening and concluding episodes fit the themes of the novel.

2. The proverb proper is one of the most philosophical of Igbo aesthetic media, and the conventions of the genre constitute a safeguard, a medium for the conveyance in telling phrases of the principles for successful living too deep for direct, undisguised expression. Discussion can focus on the dimensions of spectacle they convey, the sometimes amusing or humorous or satiric or caustically or gently lampooning but always vivid and captivating stories they tell.

3. In keeping with the *egwugwu*'s function as a regulating and ordering instrument, a power it's invested in by both the gods and the human community, is the figure of the mask worn by *egwugwu* in which that power is enshrined. Relating the disguise conveyed by masking to the concept of artisitic license, the immunity art confers for social regulation can lead to the discovery of one of the most important roles Achebe's Igbo society attaches to art.

4. The embedded narrative, the story-within-the-story, or anecdote, otherwise known as narrative-proverb, can profitably be described as characterized by elegance and self-sufficiency. It is a dynamic mode of expression. Exploring the source of the energy of this form of fictional technique as utilized in this novel can lead to intellectually stimulating reading.

STUDY QUESTIONS

1. Embedded narrative devices – anecdotes, animal fables, folktales, song-tales, proverbs, ballads, myths and proverbs – show the extent to which *Things Fall Apart*'s representational method has been stretched to accommodate the minimalist narrative

criteria, as this chapter's treatment of the style of the novel has indicated. Locate some examples of these devices, other than those mentioned, which are featured in *Things Fall Apart*, and describe what they contribute to the specific episodes in which they are inscribed and the overall stylistic and thematic structure of the novel.

2. What are the benefits and drawbacks that unavoidably attend the use of the unidentified narrator in *Things Fall Apart*? What would the story gain and/or lose if it were told by a different narrative method – for example, by participant narrators (Okonkwo, Unoka, Obierika, Amalinze the Cat, Ezeulu, Okonkwo's wives, Ezinma, or the District Commissioner)? (You may find a handle around this question by rewriting episodes from the novel from the viewpoints of any of these characters – for example, the opening story of the wrestling contest narrated by the defeated Amalinze the Cat.)

3. Examine in reasonable detail what the ethnographic method contributes to *Things Fall Apart* by focusing on specific episodes – for instance, the feast of the New Yam in Chapter 5 or the conduct of Ezeulu's funeral in Chapter 10 – and exploring how these scenes utilize anecdotes or proverbs, as the case may be, to unfold, reiterate or reinforce the themes of the passages.

CHAPTER 3

READING *THINGS FALL APART*: THE COMMUNAL WORLD, THE EMBATTLED ZONES OF CONQUEST, AND THE DECLINE OF TRADITION

Of the many richly detailed fictionalized accounts of the texture of African communal life and of the onset of European imperial encroachment into it, *Things Fall Apart*'s are the most sparkling and most complex. In this book, one of the classics of literary ethnography – indeed one of the novels that define what traditional Africa is – author Achebe's sensitivity and thoroughness convey to readers a pre-colonial world of the Igbos of Nigeria, making scene after scene reveal spectacular information about the quotidian social life of two of their communities. *Things Fall Apart* creates a crystalline view of Igbo customs, including family life in the polygamous household, the patterns of falling in love and marriage, work and play in the public communal setting, and the placement of women in this patriarchal society. Even within its modest and compressed form, Achebe's novel presents an astonishing wealth of materials and close attention to detail about the seasonal rhythm of the year and the intense interest the Igbos have in going about earning a living, making sense of their existence, governing themselves, and burying their dead, all of which the novel uses to reveal the complex particularities of their attitudes and values as a distinct cultural group. In this way, the account of the genesis of European missionary and military invasion of that world that accompanies the story falls naturally into place as an exploration of a powerful force that came to upset the many layers of harmony that an African people know and love.

Any text as popular and layered as *Things Fall Apart* is bound to be read and re-read in a number of different ways in the light of ever developing insights and perspectives.[1] Thematically, approaches taken so far in readings of the novel fall into two distinct camps. There are, on the one hand, those who read the novel as the story of

Okonkwo, a famous warrior and expert farmer who rises quickly from humble origins to become a wealthy and respected leader of his clan only to fall precipitously from those heights.[2] In these readings, the novel is thought of as being about the deeds of an impressive individual. With an emphatic critical focus placed on the centrality of the super-sized image of Okonkwo and his human weaknesses and strengths, what emerges is a view of the world in which the individual is conceived as the primary agent of change in society, the controller of both his and society's destiny.

Those who view the novel as essentially the story of a community, on the other hand, do acknowledge the fact that hero Okonkwo's destiny intertwines with his people's.[3] Distinguishing their reading, however, is a belief that an interest in peoples' lives quite apart from their community makes one liable to brush over the determinist laws of historical change which make us understand that human beings are largely what society makes them. At the heart of this method of reading is the image of people as both objects and subjects of change. Though people act and are acted upon in time and place by their surroundings, this view upholds, the burden of the force of history is ultimately corporately borne by communities. When carefully examined, it will be clear that each of these points of view is right in stressing those features of the text to which it gives attention, but both gain in magnitude and importance when they are considered together because neither is, strictly speaking, correct alone.

Both perceptions of the novel can work closely and collaboratively together for good reason: *Things Fall Apart*'s density makes it nearly infinitely suggestive: it is meaningful on many levels: Framed by two interlocking plots, the Okonkwo family plot and his Umofia and Mbanta communities' plot, the two worlds inevitably intersect with one another. Although it is written in the realistic mode, *Things Fall Apart* has symbolic resonances. Its multi-layered design enables it to perform the two main functions that Thomas H. Luxon has identified with allegories: the ability 'to forge a figural view of reality while championing the "literal" and "historical"'.[4] In the same context, Luxon finds in allegorical presentation a tendency for 'text and reality' to 'exchange and re-exchange positions' (1995: 29). Achebe is not included in that study, which is primarily concerned with the English Reformation, but the process Luxon observes is applicable to *Things Fall Apart* for while, on one hand, Achebe's characters are clearly fictional creations, on the other, the material contents of his text (European colonialism and the Igbo response to it) are well-known factual events in African social history which are verifiable from both written records and the oral tradition.

To recognize *Things Fall Apart* as a political allegory in a pastoral mode is to discover that it is a novel as much about what happens in moral and spiritual terms as about the outcome of the political events it depicts. The text's main focus centres on the threat to Igbo sovereignity and other aspects of the rural culture of the people. That pressure includes menace to Igbo religious traditions and ideas of good and evil as well. As a specific form of allegory, the exemplum, *Things Fall Apart* has a double function: to show an active illustration of traditional African culture in all its vibrancy and to highlight the fallout resulting from its destabilization by European imperial expansion.

Despite these modest objectives, *Things Fall Apart* confronts readers with a series of enigmas. Principally, its deceptive simplicity hides a complex thematic and stylistic texture. It begins with the simple story of tragic hero Okonkwo. But it uses Okonkwo's career to show how the individual's fate and the destiny of his community are collapsed into one another. As a result, Umofia and Mbanta, the representative Igbo communities highlighted, emerge not as mere backdrops for the exploration of Okonkwo's personal dilemmas but as the definitive pictures of the unified order of the historical Igbo society in the period between 1890 and 1900 when the British presence began to establish itself in the region.

MALE ACTS, FEMALE SPECTATORSHIP: DISSOLVING BORDERS THROUGH THE DEMOCRACY OF SPORTS

To properly understand this compressed novel, the reader should be very attentive to the subtextual issues raised right from the very opening scene of the famous extraordinary wrestling match, in which the underdog fighter Okonkwo makes history by overthrowing the reigning champion of his region. In that important textual moment, an encounter of epic proportions takes place. It's certainly not a mere coincidence that Achebe opens and closes his novel with combat. It is the unifying thread in the novel. The momentous, fierce wrestling contest at the beginning, with different twists of plots, in which society is caught up in a frenzy of anticipation that quickly terminates with the sudden breathtaking victory of the courageous rising star, is indicative of the uncommon promise with which Okonkwo begins his career and the energy of the community which it is his good fortune to have behind him, though he ends up disappointingly not being able to take adequate advantage of it. The bloodier, more violent conflict that wraps up the story, in which a life is taken leading to the annihilation of the cultural hero himself by the very hands with which he secured the reputed wrestling victory at his first battle in the novel's opening scene, suggests a round defeat, the grave disappointment of the monumental initial promise of Okonkwo's career and the agony of his community that had its bubbling expectations deflated within the twinkle of an eye and can only helplessly watch the ecstatic victorious British colonial order making away with the real trophy.

What these key opening and closing textual moments show is that fighting is central to *Things Fall Apart*'s plan to capture a world exhaustively detailed with events which make up an Igbo people's mundane grind of daily existence and seasonal cycle of occurrences. Fighting also carries a huge symbolic significance that is integral to the novel's overall structure; after all, it is the enabling event that permits hero Okonkwo to stand out among his peers at the beginning, and it is also the decisive force that brings him down in the end. Donatus Nwoga (1964) recognized quite early the importance of Okonkwo's struggle with his *chi*, his guardian angel or fate. Ironically, the component of Okonkwo's struggle that has even more to say about *Things Fall Apart*'s organizing principle of structure, the part to do with the function assigned to fighting, is the part readers have not yet commented upon, though it is even more important.

Achebe opens his novel with a fight in part to provide readers with a graphic image of the impending cultural struggle in the realm of the word, a linguistic tussle between English as the language of authority and the subject Igbo language. There are few things worse than a confrontation of unequally matched forces; for the indigenous African languages the collision with European languages is something of a lost cause from the start. According to Loreto Todd, when European and African languages came into contact with each other, jostling for supremacy caused 'the relexification' of the 'mother tongue' of Africans, whose writers were then forced to use 'English vocabulary but indigeneous structures and rhythms' (1982: 303). It is a fate Chantal Zabus calls one of 'domination' of African languages by European languages (1991: 104). Presented in Igbo-inflected English, *Things Fall Apart* can be seen as an instance of this process of linguistic hybridization, in which victory for English obviously translates into a corresponding marginalization for Igbo.

Things Fall Apart opens with a furious fight also as a ploy to provide an anchor for a major formula: to make tangible the subject of the impending violent military attack by European forces and of Okonkwo's signifying leadership role in the response by the anti-colonial forces of liberation. In this way, not only does the narrative foreshadow two of the novel's predominant themes, but it also quite appropriately begins by portraying Okonkwo as a figure of historical transition, a superman who is physically an imposing symbol of strength, though we soon realize that he is crumbling from within; the edifice of a declining old order confronting the emergent colonial hegemonic one:[5]

> Okonkwo was well known throughout the nine villages and even beyond. His fame rested on solid personal achievements. As a young man of eighteen he had brought honour to his village by throwing Amalinze the Cat. Amalinze was the great wrestler who for seven years was unbeaten, from Umofia to Mbaino. He was called the Cat because his back would never touch the earth. It was this man that Okonkwo threw in a fight which the old man agreed was one of the fiercest since the founder of their town engaged a spirit of the wild for seven nights.
>
> The drums beat and the flutes sang and the spectators held their breath. Amalinze was a wily craftsman, but Okonkwo was as slippery as a fish in water. Every nerve and every muscle stood out on their arms, on their backs and their thighs, and one almost heard them stretching to breaking point. In the end Okonkwo threw the Cat.[6]

As readers often agree, individual accomplishment is the cornerstone of the Igbo social life depicted in the novel. In the intensely patriarchal culture of the Igbos, no man wants to be invisible; every man wants recognition. This is the force that impels each man to strive for something to make him break out of the lot, to rise above the rank and file.[7] When Okonkwo executes the finishing wrestling manoeuvre and puts to rout his legendary opponent, he activates that principle and communicates the certain urgency he feels to outperform everyone. At least from the outside looking in, he looks strong. And it is apparent that, since the same drive has made the seven villages of the Umofia clan to be so 'powerful in war and in magic' that its 'priests and medicine-men' are 'feared' in the region (8), the narrative is distinctly touting the men as those exclusively invested with agency. Right from the foundational episode, this novel appears to deny any form of instrumentality to the female gender.

Yet a closer attention reveals that things are more complex than they at first appear. In fact, the women are not to be dismissed as mere spectators or idle bystanders since they take an active interest in gearing up the men as they flex their muscles. It would be wrong to equate male performance with power, and female spectatorship with passiveness. Contrary to what some critics maintain, we cannot definitively and restrictively associate men with the centre and women with the margins in this novel. Even the events pitching Okonkwo against Amalinze the Cat indicate that the epic battle is as much the concern of the spectators, who are mostly women and children, as it is that of the two male contestants.[8] And, since Okonkwo is not as strong as he looks from the outside, the essence of manhood may not be what it is perceived to be either, if he is considered to define it.

There are hardly any sporting events where audiences do not have major impacts on the outcomes of the contest, usually through their applause or boos and jeers. It is no surprise that the traditional Igbo wrestling event is no different. Primarily because the viewing publics have a visibly intimidating affective presence, the battle for victory here, as in any other sporting event, is as much the story of spectator involvement as it is that of the personal efforts of the men who are embroiled in the contest of wills. This audience participation is registered by the way the uncertainty of the contest's outcome is presented as though it were as much a cause of anxiety for the men locking horns as it is for the deeply engaged viewers of the progress of the fight. The result of the fight is the drawing board of the event. Thus, there are no indifferent bystanders. No wonder, when Okonkwo outfoxes the fox himself and secures eventual victory, it is received as much as a notch on his belt as it is a triumph for his supporters who have set great store by it. Wrestling fans, one of the most ardent of whom is evidently Okonkwo's own wife Ekwefi, make such a huge emotional investment in the fight it can be said that victory is secured from the very palpable energy of the crowd. That is why there are hardly any audience members who are indifferent about the result of the fight.

Because the great admiration for Okonkwo which the Umofia society expresses at the opening of the novel is tied to his heroic fighting trophy, it is inconceivable that without the wrestling event he would build the impressive career credited to him. It is a fait accompli that the Igbo wrestling audience is an audience acutely aware of its own relevance, an audience with a consciousness of its own significance, of the power of its fervour. By occasioning his meteoric rise to fame and eminence, Okonkwo's wrestling accolade inserts itself into the heart of the novel's design, not only in structural and stylistic terms, in the way great novels often utilize finely etched opening scenes to keep the reader in suspense, but also in terms of summing up their subject matter to relax the tension.

Thematically, Okonkwo's dauntless victory against Amalinze the Cat and the cheers it has drawn stand apart as a testament of successful communal endeavour, casting all his other efforts into doubt and relative insignificance. Here is the only event where the ill-fated protagonist achieves total victory, an achievement that brings both himself and all his community a totalizing sense of fulfilment and is widely celebrated as such. The realization of a democratic ideal, a concept dear to the Igbos, Okonkwo's gallant wrestling feat is a grand illustration of the belief that by taking the apparent failure of one's family as a spur to boost one's drive to want more of life, one can overturn what the family did to bring one down and cripple one's soul by doing the opposite of what is expected of someone from one's family. It thus stands here for a man's ability to overcome any event that challenges his mettle and pushes him beyond both his physical and mental limitations.

It is therefore an event with resonant structural and thematic implications for the meaning of the narrative, offering the lesson that just as mere brute force is not the primary arsenal employed in defeating Amalinze the Cat, combating British imperial designs effectively will require more than brute force; it will need the kind of deft tactics employed by Okonkwo in securing a win. Through the transformation it undergoes in the hands of the novelist, the valiant wrestling competition moves from being just a game of personal rivalry into a communal contest of wills. The wrestling contest offers a uniquely appropriate metaphor for understanding the colonization/decolonization antithesis, because its import is not lost on the audience; the Igbos are a competitive people so they are no strangers to contention against obstacles. Since they lived in a setting where accolades lingered long in the cultural memory of society, the wrestling event and the victory it confers carried a greater gravitas of effect in their society than it would in the information overload culture of today, where successive floods of events seem to overwhelm society with uncanny rapidity and vanish out of the communal memory just as quickly as they occur.

What is evident, then, it is important to pause to notice, is the subtle way in which the novel puts a symbolical political spin on the dialectic of the sporting event, for with a single stroke it delineates the type of dexterity the Igbos will need to defeat European occupation forces. Of course, by the end of this novel, as in the true history it represents, the plan to mount a triumphant native resistance to colonization turns out to be a pipe dream, since it happens that Okonkwo's slaying of the court messenger doesn't galvanize his people's united action to resist the occupation forces as he had hoped. He ends up hanging himself. The community that celebrated his victory at the wrestling encounter is now left even without the voice to mourn. 'That man was one of the greatest men in Umofia', the community's spokesman, Obierika, quietly and ruefully tells the District Commissioner. 'You drove him to kill himself; and now he will be buried like a dog . . .' (147).

The focus of Obierika's moving private remarks expresses his clear vision of the importance of audience participation, of communal involvement with the individual's experience. The main focus of his grief is that at his best friend's death his community cannot even do his body its last duty. Tradition forbids the Umofia and Mbanta people to touch the body of a suicide. And so, Obierika asks the white District Commissioner to take it. The tragic isolation of the community leader's final moments is summed up by the figures of the villagers walking away from his dangling body and the image of the District Commissioner himself walking back to the court with his thoughts focused not on planning a funeral that would be befitting of the stature of the deceased but on the trivial matter of writing a book of memoirs in which 'the story of a man who killed a messenger and then hanged himself' might take up 'perhaps not a whole chapter but a reasonable paragraph, at any rate' (147–8).

Without anyone ready to receive his body, Okonkwo becomes an abandoned man. The District Commissioner appears to make a comedy of the eventual defeat this means for Okonkwo. But for the community, Okonkwo's demise is no laughing matter at all; rather, it is a matter with implications that lie beyond his personal elimination: a communal disaster for Igboland in material terms because nothing in Umofia's history before this event compares with the collective sense of horror that has been unleashed by the disaster. It signals the complete end of the old order in Igboland as a whole. Indeed, the monumental scope of the crisis that the event of Okonkwo's death has fomented is marked for the reader by the terrifying appearances which it has summoned to life, an acme of confusion and disorder:

> That night the Mother of the Spirits walked the length and breadth of the clan, weeping for her murdered son. It was a terrible night. Not even the oldest man in Umofia had ever heard such a strange and fearful sound, and it was never to be heard again. It seemed as if the very soul of the tribe wept for a great evil that was coming – its own death.
>
> On the next day all the masked *egwugwu* of Umofia assembled in the market-place. They came from all the quarters of the clan and even from the neighbouring villages. The dreaded Otakagu came from Imo, and Ekwensu, dangling a white cork, arrived from Uli. It was a terrible gathering. The eerie voices of countless spirits, the bells that clattered behind some of them, and the clash of matchets as they ran forwards and backwards and saluted one another, sent tremors of fear into every heart. For the first time in living memory the sacred bull-roarer was heard in broad daylight. (132)

The pressures that society now feels and senses are so new and so threatening that it cannot yet name them. Just as he did in life, in his death Okonkwo has acted in ways that have called forth a big story. Yet, big as the story of his wrestling victory undeniably is, being the one event that established his initial designation as warrior and ultimate fighting machine, the story of Okonkwo's death has even more far-reaching impact in at least one respect: unlike the glory of his wrestling prize – uproarious as it is – his death is no ordinary event. In fact, in a reversal of his open victory that is a major subject of public celebration at the novel's opening scene, Okonkwo's death signals that instead of his being in command of the situation, someone else is; instead of being surrounded by admiring, cheering audiences or grieving relatives, Okonkwo is a man publicly unmourned; a man who has left his community to stand silent and separated. This is the sense in which his defeat fits neatly into the combat pattern of the novel's narrative frame, serving as it does as a closure to a major chapter of Igbo history. Okonkwo may have had the first word on victory, but it is the British who have the last.[9]

AGRICULTURE, RANK, AND THE CULT OF RECOGNITION: SOCIAL CLIMBING AND THE FUTILITY OF THE QUEST

Even if only for the fascinating story it tells about a strong male desire among the Igbos – a near-chivalric type ambition embodied in a frantic search for social capital – Okonkwo's desperate struggle to earn seed yams, the first major battle he has to overcome after posting victory at the famous wrestling combat, repays detailed attention. It is also epochal in another respect: it bears much resemblance to Europe's empire-building quests and is thus a feature that adds to the artistic integrity of the novel, for it demonstrates clearly that just as Britain rose to power by plundering the mineral wealth of Africa, the spices of Asia, and the trades of the Middle East, Okonkwo has to count on authority to rub off on him not by marrying an emperor's daughter as we have it in chivalric romances but by connecting with someone who has 'three huge barns, nine wives and thirty children' and has taken 'the highest but one title which a man could take in the clan' (13–14).

Okonkwo, having convinced himself that he started life with the disadvantage of not getting the inheritance of 'a barn' or a young wife from his father, therefore makes a last-ditch decision to visit a wealthy man in his village to borrow seed yams with which he hopes to achieve that much-needed break. In practical terms, however, just as expanding territorial domains and authority never comes about without pain (expansionist imperial Britain had to fight battles with unpredictable climates and dangerous terrains), so rising to wealth and local power will not be handed to Okonkwo on a golden platter. Okonkwo has tougher battles ahead, since getting paramount citizenship would require him to be first reduced to a *persona non grata*. Okonkwo must first pay his dues by submitting himself for the honour set before him; he has to lay down his pride to take it up again in greater measure. He must first forfeit the very dignity eminence will confer and show a willingness to endure short-term discomforts for the gratification that lies ahead.

The somewhat paradoxical idea reflected in Okonkwo's career is that the road to public honour is paved with insults of a private kind. The image of Okonkwo going down on his knees before Nwakibie tells it all – a man abasing himself before another man:

> He took a pot of palm-wine and a cock to Nwakibie. Two elderly neighbours were sent for, and Nwakibie's two grown-up sons were also present in his *obi*. He presented a kola nut and an alligator pepper, which was passed round for all to see and then returned to him . . .
>
> After the kola nut had been eaten Okonkwo brought his palm-wine from the corner of the hut where it had been placed and stood it in the centre of the group. He addressed Nwakibie, calling him 'our father'.
>
> '*Nna ayi*', he said. 'I have brought you this little kola. As our people say, a man who pays respect to the great paves the way for his own greatness. I have come to pay you my respects and also to ask for a favour. But let us drink the wine first.' (14)

The testimony offered by such clues as the deferential acts of presenting Nwakibie with 'a pot of palm-wine and a cock', 'a kola nut and an alligator pepper', and of adopting the appropriate mode of address for a dignitary of his calibre by calling Nwakibie 'our father' is significant. Indeed, it is noteworthy that Okonkwo's obeisant outlook is not all that different from the comely way in which Nwakibie's own wives present themselves before his awe-inspiring presence. Unlike the way in which the women in the traditional Igbo polygamous household typically carry themselves with a certain stately bearing, Nwakibie's wives exhibit behaviour more in keeping with that of a harem in a non-egalitarian set-up. Thus, after the usual exchange of niceties and pleasantries, when the palm-wine is shared among the men present, Nwakibie calls in his wives and they enter in their order of seniority, get down on one knee, drink, and then walk away.

There must be something going on inside Okonkwo that makes him show a similar servile complaisance, for when the business resumes, this is how he pronounces his mission:

'I have come for your help,' he said. 'Perhaps you can already guess what it is. I have cleared a farm but have no yams to sow. I know what it is to ask a man to trust another with his yams, especially these days when young men are afraid of hard work. I am not afraid of work. The lizard that jumped from the high iroko tree to the ground said he would praise himself if no one else did. I began to fend for myself when most people still suck at their mothers' breasts. If you give me some yam seeds I shall not fail you.' (15–16)

In contrast to Okonkwo's self-effacing presentation, Nwakibie exults in being feted because it is the appropriate behaviour for social dignitaries in his community that observes a rarefied sense of rank. Thus, he boasts heartily to the gathering that he has turned down many similar requests from other young men because he knows 'they would just dump them in the earth and leave them to be choked by weeds' (16). Justifying his action as not arising out of heartlessness but out of adaptation to experience, he says he has learnt from Eneke the bird who 'says that since men have learnt to shoot without missing, he has learnt to fly without perching' (16). So Nwakibie tells Okonkwo that he has learnt 'to be stingy' with his yams. 'But I can trust you. I know it as I look at you. As our fathers said, you can tell a ripe corn by its look. I shall give you twice four hundred yams. Go ahead and prepare your farm.' (16)

As testified by the power of the proverbs used by both of these speakers to clarify their positions during that sensitive and tactful conversation, the burden of interest is upon the manner in which Okonkwo has conducted himself so far as a supplicant presenting a delicate and heavy request before an authority figure. The matter of the award of credit is a weighty one, and so composure is everything, for it is the manner of Okonkwo's disposition that will make the difference between having his petition heard or rejected like those of the other young men who tried before him. Though simmering with haughtiness, Okonkwo therefore comes to Nwakibie cloaked in the garb of humility. Thanks to the power of one's bearing to lubricate human relations among the Igbos, Nwakibie gives up his seed yams because of the apparent humility of Okonkwo's demeanour ('I know it as I look at you').

The bitter irony of this whole episode in Okonkwo's life is that the damage has already been done both to his mental frame and to his emotional poise. The ethical tone of Nwakibie's speech suggests that he censures many young men who 'come to ask for yams' because he considers appearance to be a decided index of character, and rituals of power as unspoken, hidden public transcripts require poor people to acknowledge their lowly status with politeness. When Okonkwo accepts this hierarchy – Nwakibie's open display of domination – therefore, he earns the rich man's assistance. Thus 'Okonkwo thanked him again and again and went home feeling happy. He knew that Nwakibie would not refuse him, but he had not expected he would be so generous' (16).

In *Domination and the Arts of Resistance*, James C. Scott observes that 'members of the dominant groups . . . learn the knack of acting with authority and self-assurance from socialization. For hereditary ruling groups the training has typically begun at birth; the aristocrat learns how to act like an aristocrat, the Brahim like a Brahim, the man like a man. For those whose position is not inherited, on-the-job training is required to make them convincing in their roles as bosses, professors, military officers, colonial officials' (1992: 49). As a result, Scott adds that, to survive, poor people have to learn to act appropriate conduct by employing devices of concealment, to hide their true feelings in their relations with the powerful.

It is not surprising that Okonkwo's joy is short-lived. It turns out that his visit to Nwakibie is a clear instance of the sort of discomfiting situation described by Scott, one in which a poor person is compelled by circumstances beyond his control to seek out the rich and powerful. That is why, in consonance with the kinds of circumspect behaviour expected in such settings, Okonkwo has no choice but to humble himself. Borrowing seed yams from Nwakibie finally brings him face to face with the situation he has dreaded and tried hard to avoid all along: becoming a debtor like his own father, Unoka.

The borrowing of seed yams is one of those ambivalent acts which on one level leverages Okonkwo's material base, yet on another level questions, and even undermines, his confidence. Somewhat subliminally, whether or not Okonkwo himself is aware of it, becoming a debtor serves as a physical reinforcement of the mental violations he has already suffered through his acceptance of the sense of the inferiority of his patrimony. The manner of getting the seed yams eventuates a significant psychological slide for Okonkwo. A victim of economic assault, he is first a victim of psychological abuse, a brutalization which the process of earning the seed yams only incenses.

A mentally self-undermining act, a deed with a strategy of persuasion that falls short of achieving the desired result of building Okonkwo up, that visit contains a stirring critique of the motive force of its own success because the results that it brings are mixed: though successful in getting Okonkwo the seed yams, the visit comes with a heavy price, not just producing the opposite result of what was intended by lowering his confidence even further, but also causing him to lose perhaps the last shred of the most precious asset he could possibly have as a man, especially at that formative stage of his life: his relationship with his own father, the very foundation on which a man's sense of security is based.

Had it not transformed Okonkwo into a snob, intensifying his disregard of his own father, Okonkwo's association with Nwakibie would not have been as damaging as it turns out to be. Because a young man needs a father to validate him, Okonkwo's holding his father in low regard ultimately takes away from him that key pillar of parental love and security, the ingedients of inner peace and wholesomeness known as self-dignity.

James Scott rightly argues a few pages further on in the same book that dignity is 'at once a very private and a very public attribute' (1992: 113). One can therefore become diminished, or as Scott puts it nicely in the same context, '[one] can experience indignity at the hands of another despite the fact that no one else sees or hears about it. What is reasonably clear, however, is that any indignity is compounded greatly when it is inflicted in public' (113). This explanation is not inapposite for understanding the far-reaching negative psychological effects that Okonkwo's consort with Nwakibie causes him, especially in light of Scott's remark that '[an] insult, a look of contempt, a physical humiliation, an assault on one's character and standing, a rudeness is nearly always far more injurious when it is inflicted before an audience' (113).

Given Okonkwo's impressionable personality, it makes sense that his presentation before Nwakibie should fatally weaken, if not entirely eliminate, what little patrimonial regard he has left. Having to literally grovel before Nwakibie, who is surrounded by his admiring wives and the august company to which he belongs, could only have a most humbling effect on Okonkwo. Undoubtedly, the contribution of the occasion to his heightening sense of the low opinion he already has of himself cannot be overemphasized. First sparked by his believing how the public views his father, especially swallowing the opinion of his own peers wholesale, Okonkwo's sagging sense of self is brought to its climax as he sits in a stunned state at Nwakibie's feet.

Ostentation is a sign of the snob, and so all of Okonkwo's subsequent outlandish pursuit of success, which he narrowly defines to equate with material prosperity and aggression, can be seen as motivated by a desperate desire to redeem the self-inflicted insult of consorting with a superior who did not prove as nurturing as hoped. The feeling of being lesser than another person is not conducive to a sense of security; the love of oneself casts out fear; anything which lessens one's sense of self causes inner dissonance, which is why in Okonkwo's case,

> his whole life was dominated by fear, the fear of failure and of weakness. It was deeper and more intimate than the fear of evil and capricious gods and of magic, the fear of the forest, and the forces of nature, malevolent, red in tooth and claw. Okonkwo's fear was greater than these. It was not external but lay deep within himself. It was the fear of himself, lest he should be found to resemble his father. Even as a little boy he had resented his father's failure and weakness, and even now he still remembered how he had suffered when a playmate had told him that his father was *agbala*. That was how Okonkwo came to know that *agbala* was not only another name for a woman, it could also mean a man who had taken no title. And so Okonkwo was ruled by one passion – to hate everything that his father Unoka had loved. One of those things was gentleness and another was idleness. (9–10)

Perhaps if he could avoid being paranoid, Okonkwo would understand that in his society 'a man was judged according to his worth and not according to the worth of his father' (6). In any case, he might also form an independent opinion of his own father regarding other attributes like compassion, taste, integrity, friendliness, intelligence and creativeness. Perhaps if Okonkwo was not so blinded by his own narrow personal agenda, he might notice that he has a good father. Unoka possesses several sterling qualities. Surprisingly, Okonkwo gives little thought to the encouragement his father offers him during the 'terrible harvest month' that followed the year he borrowed the seed yams from Nwakibie. 'Do not despair', Unoka tells his son, at that moment of great depression. 'I know you will not despair. You have a manly and a proud heart. A proud heart can survive a general failure because such a failure does not prick its pride. It is more difficult and more bitter when a man fails alone' (18). Far from being the bumbling idiot Okonkwo makes him out to be, Unoka's words suggest that he is rather more of a sage who is as eager as he is determined to build up his son. A paradox in Okonkwo's behaviour is that his overcompensating masculinity, which is really his manner of covering up a low self-esteem, causes him to despise his own father, a man whose image he cannot bear and wants to eradicate as if it were a deadly virus.

As well as being a coward, and a tender-hearted person who could not hurt a fly, Unoka took no titles and was saddled with a heavy burden of debt and harassed incessantly by creditors. But he was not stupid. Rather, he was a highly learned man, who received a lesson or two from the field in which he was better than anyone, his musical career, which he could have passed on in his family – especially to Okonkwo. Okonkwo misjudges his own father because of his mis-placed ambitions that triggered the paranoid fear of being in danger of inheriting a bad image. Fear is the emotion that causes him to lose the sense of balance of things, which not only has the undermining effect of depriving him of personal inner peace but also causes the ever-escalating tensions in his relationships with others. While youthful exuberance draws Okonkwo into trouble, the material for temperate judgement already exists within his reach were he to look to the lessons of his own wrestling success, which is grounded in the value of negotiating delicate situations with extreme adroitness and graceful resolve and of learning to avoid the easy routes of abrasion and to take the more complex ones.

Nowhere is the scenario better played out than in the case of Unoka: that a discrepancy could exist between how a person looks or what people think of him, on the one hand, and who he really is on the other. It is particularly the case in a rural setting, such as Unoka's, which is perennially rife with circulating misconceived ideas about neighbours, that the image people have of one another can be based on suspect theorizing, a combination of truths and half-truths: conjectures, speculations, rumours, slander and gossip. It is quite natural that characterizations of Unoka have been in line with these sorts of practice. Culled from a mixture of truths, half-truths and plain exaggerations accepted and circulated by a public that has not bothered to make any effort to get to the bottom of things by way of painstaking in-depth analysis, opinions about Unoka beg to be taken with a grain of salt:

> In his day he was lazy and improvident and was quite incapable of thinking about tomorrow. If any money came his way, and it seldom did, he immediately bought gourds of palm-wine, called round his neighbours and made merry. He always said that whenever he saw a dead man's mouth he saw the folly of not eating what one had in one's lifetime. Unoka was, of course, a debtor, and he owed every neighbour some money, from a few cowries to quite substantial amounts.
>
> He was tall but very thin and had a slight stoop. He wore a haggard and mournful look except when he was drinking or playing on his flute. He was very good on his flute, and his happiest moments were the two or three moons after the harvest when the village musicians brought down their instruments, hung above the fireplace. Unoka would play with them, his face beaming with blessedness and peace. (3–4)

It is through the contrasting personalities of Okonkwo and his father Unoka that Achebe gets the chance to explore the gap between appearance and reality. People generally think of Unoka as lazy and improvident, but the absence of definitive attribution in the statements in circulation about him reflects the lack of truth-value assigned to each one of those claims by the narrative, claims that derive more from the common lore of hearsay than from verifiable evidence: that he is 'quite incapable of thinking about tomorrow'; 'He always said that whenever he saw a dead man's mouth he saw the folly'; 'He wore a haggard and mournful look except when he was drinking'.

On the contrary, the real truth is that Unoka is financially insecure, but this is not because he lacks either talent or the drive to enlarge his estate. Rather, it is indicated that Unoka could not make a decent living from his craft because he lives and works as a musician in a setting where the musical profession has not gained commercial value. Though he is suspected of having such an inclination, far from being lazy, Unoka is a very hard-working man. A musical celebrity who is the life of the party in his community, Unoka has brought more joy to many than anyone and has made a huge investment in the entertainment industry in his society. This is the reason that he is portrayed in an essentially positive light by the narrative.[10] It is not without good reason that Unoka's musical skills were in high demand around neighbouring villages, where he took great delight and effort in mentoring fledgling musicians and dancers: 'Unoka loved the good fare and the good fellowship (4).

One may question whether it is Unoka's choice to belong to 'that class of artists who believe that they should live for their work and not prostitute the integrity of their art to sterile materialism' (Palmer, 1972: 56). There is simply not enough evidence to show that Unoka is a rebel in revolt against the trappings of material wealth; what we are shown, however, is that he has the reputation his musical talent conferred on him but lacks financial substance or political authority in his society because the profession of the artist has not yet gained commercial viability. In any event, it does not make any sense to expect someone as mired in debt as Unoka is to disapprove of additional income.

One reason for being misjudged and suspected of having inclinations to be lazy is that Unoka is the kind of person who is as happy as a lark. Perfectly in tune with nature, Unoka makes merry when the weather is good, for example, when old men and children would 'sit round log fires, warming bodies', he 'loved it all, and he loved the first kites that returned with the dry season, and the children who sang songs of welcome to them. He would remember his own childhood, how he had often wandered around looking for a kite sailing leisurely against the blue sky. As soon as he found one he would sing with his whole being, welcoming it back from its long, long journey, and asking it if it had brought home any lengths of cloth' (4). Some people think his relaxed mood a form of laziness. But that isn't quite correct. Unoka simply has a laid-back personality. His attitude of not taking life too seriously (he keeps looking for amusement) and his leisurely lifestyle are functional in that they give his community the drama of fun, humour, and love and pleasure, a touch of light-heartedness it badly lacks. As happens to Okonkwo, if anyone gets dismissive of Unoka's good nature, the knack of frivolity he embodies, such an individual does so at his or her own peril.

A figure of fun, Unoka is undeniably one of *Things Fall Apart*'s most influential characters, about whom readers have only a limited knowledge even though he is central to the plot's overall structure. After all, it is he who helps Achebe to sound forth the theme of the tranquility of Igbo tribal life, of the motif of primordial innocence, of the period when Igbos had a oneness not only with themselves but also with nature and lived a stress-free life. Considering that Unoka is an essentially agreeable man, it is as though the unspoken or implied idea suggested by his not getting along easily with his own son Okonkwo is that there is a hidden problem somewhere.[11] Readers of the novel come face to face with one reality: in the social embarrassment or humiliation and shame that Okonkwo feels over his sense that his father is worthless, in Okonkwo's snobbery and overweening self-regard and his frantic search to repair this apparently irremediable status he believes he has inherited, one enters into the world of a hypertensive megalomaniac, a world in which the dichotomy between the society's success code and the sense an over-ambitious but wounded hero has of it looms large, a world that does not lack the touch of the theatrical.

During his confinement within this shabby world, becoming a successful farmer, becoming the holder of multiple titles and owner of a big household filled with multiple wives – none of these things can bring Okonkwo any more lasting satisfaction than the public applause of his larger-than-life wrestling performance when he won a monumental victory over Amalinze the Cat did, given the voraciousness of his ambitions. Depicting him as a man in bondage to an idea of unattainable success, a man doing hard time for the disturbed conditions of elemental discontent and of being lost and not knowing who he is, the narrative shows clearly why, with his vision of achievement set so firmly on a narrow conception of his society's parameters of accomplishment, so many things are bound to go badly wrong in Okonkwo's relationships and judgements; for despite the absence of bars and shackles, Okonkwo has found himself in a virtual prison, doing time behind the walls of his own consciousness, trapped behind the walls of self-imprisonment to a misplaced idea of ultimate self-fulfilment.

In his lucid analysis of the novel, critic Chidi Okonkwo refers readers to the fact that the protagonist 'lives by a warped code of exaggerated masculinity dictated by his own neurotic personality, a perversion of cultural ideals in the past and a dangerous anachronism in the present' (1999: 120).[12] Hero Okonkwo's behaviour leaves no doubt about the stiff opposition his singular perspective poses to 'Umofia's success ethic [that] is predicated upon a complementarity of masculine and feminine values (the so-called male and female principles)' (120). These dualities of which Okonkwo remains tragically oblivious are embodied, the critic adds,

> in the elaborate ritual balancing of the three cosmic planes of female Earth, male Sky and the spiritual doman; patrilineal, warlike Umofia's dependence on a female deity (Ani or Earth, the earth godess) as its principal deity and this deity's emanation (Agadi Nwayi or Old Woman) as source of its military prowess; the assignment of priestesses to male deities and priests to female deities; the designation of the powerful male oracle, served by the priestess Chielo, by the name Agbala which is also a designation for women and effeminate men; and the practice of burying a married woman among her own rather than her husband's kindred. In the tale of the quarrel between Earth and Sky, harmony is restored only when Earth's emissary softens Sky's heart with a song (p. 38). Such songs represent the 'poetry' of life which Achebe symbolically associates with the female principle, and Okonkwo's repudiation of this principle marks him out as a doomed man right from the beginning of the novel. (Okonkwo, 1999: 120)

The Igbos have a complex rather than a one-dimensional view of the world. But hero Okonkwo doesn't see life in its intrinsic constitutive dualities, in its binary oppositions that require a delicate balancing act of negotiation. He misjudges things to the extent that his militant and inflexible search for respectability, a vision of which he had seen when he threw Amalinze the Cat in the celebrated wrestling match, his conception of crowning success as 'exaggerated masculinity', finally crowds out the viability of other codes of values like compassion, affection, love, gentleness, cooperation, humility, tenderness, generosity, patience, tolerance, amiability, play and fun, moderation and sensitivity. This places him on a collision course with the vital life-sustaining beliefs and practices of his society. In this state, displays of emotion of every kind – except when they involve excessive manliness, rigidity, brute force, vanity, intolerance and brash treatment of those apparently less successful than himself – are shown to be either unappealing or inaccessible to him.

Though the society of the Igbos has enough flexibility to allow room for individuals like Unoka, therefore, Okonkwo's inability to overcome the overwhelming pressure to attain his tapering vision of honour predisposes him to a narrow definition of accomplishment that makes it impossible for him to have a different regard for his father. It is impossible to follow the story of Okonkwo's intense struggle for status without coming face to face with an ironic tangle: the more heated the search for social standing gets, the more the idea of status becomes a desperate way of covering up its real motivation. That impulse is the emptiness within his inner being that is precipitated by the insult of his father's figure. It is the main force driving Okonkwo to be everything his father was not. As a consequence, he develops an unruly passion, the egotism of going one better than everyone else, and of despising everything his father represents. He becomes a desperate man fighting for pride, a man with a lot to prove.

The matter of Okonkwo's bad social skills, of his inability to work in harmony with others, is one subject which recurs regularly in discussions of *Things Fall Apart*, and it offers quite a surprising perspective on how it is that someone who has such a proven track record in the public display of valour could fail so woefully in human relations, a terrain not customarily considered to be as difficult to negotiate. Life on the domestic sphere for workaholic Okonkwo is a near-complete disaster. Okonkwo's dramatic domestic life, for example, might have been comic were it not for the serious consequences it has. But at stake is the matter of the unhealthy addictions that frustrate an aspiring noble man's efforts to provide a nurturing environment for his wives and an upbringing appropriate to well-adjusted young men and women; the exchange of honour, civility, and delicacy that would add balance to their lives, a path beyond the vulgarity of materialism.

WOMEN'S TERRITORIAL DOMINANCE: THE DOMESTIC SPHERES, AFFECTION, COMMUNITY, FESTIVITY, SHARING, LOVE AND RITUAL

When we closely examine his portrait of women, we see that not even Achebe's talents have immunized him from being subjected to the usual charge that African male writers generally have a predilection for stereotypical depiction of female characters. Yet, in terms of their composite image, one could not hope for a more finely honed realistic portrait of women and womanhood than the one Achebe has put together in *Things Fall Apart*. [13] Unlike some of the images of rancour and divisiveness commonly associated with the women in the African polygamous household, Okonkwo's wives, for example, are far from a bickering, quarrelsome or self-centered lot. Not only do they act in ways that support the idea that a successful man's wives should participate in establishing and maintaining his social status through self-display, but forming a cohesive community of their own devoid of any form of cut-throat competitiveness, Okonkwo's wives also collectively represent a uniquely original picture of women in a traditional polygamous household whose charming personalities contrastively help to unveil the demons in their husband that threaten to tear apart an otherwise great community. But the women are in no way over-idealized, since they are painted in all their essential humanity, in a way that highlights both their weaknesses and strengths, an accomplishment in representation achieved by an accumulation of tightly connected ironies.

For instance, all three wives – Ekwefi, Ojiugo and Nwoye's mother – walk in obedience, taking orders from their husband. They are all eagerly waiting women, who serve his interests by regularly cooking and serving his meals on time, cleaning the compound, and doing all the domestic chores. In addition to providing these kinds of comfort at home, Okonkwo's wives all take active roles in the education and upbringing of their children, and, when required, in ritual. They are thus equal participants with their husband in the transmission of culture to ensure the survival of the race. They also lend him a helping hand on the farm, refraining from nagging or complaining unnecessarily about things, and appearing to derive personal pleasure and satisfaction from these functions.

In light of the sense of peace and tranquillity that fills Okonkwo's household whenever he is not around to disrupt the current with his tantrums, his wives seem the perfect co-wives. Collectively and individually, the wives habitually display unflagging loyalty and dedication. Not even the long-suffering Ekwefi, mother of an only surviving child, Ezinma, who has a reason not to identify with his dreams, does so. Even after losing one child after another, and after being nearly shot to death herself by her own husband, Ekwefi still does not turn bitter. Instead, she develops an unusual love for wrestling, his athletic passion, and her support does not waver one bit. If anything, Ekwefi's interest rises to the status of a passion, from when as a young woman she 'ran away from her husband and came to live with Okonkwo' to thirty years later, when she becomes 'a woman of forty-five who had suffered a great deal in her time' (28). It is indeed remarkable that the only intimate bedroom scene recorded involves Okonkwo's memories of his first sexual encounter with Ekwefi, which occurred the night she ran away from her previous husband to knock on his door. 'Even in those days he was not a man of many words. He just carried her into his bed and in the darkness began to feel around her waist for the loose end of her cloth' (76).

Collectively, Okonkwo's three wives are so respectful of the gender order, they do nothing to derail it, and their commitment to helping him sustain his public image seldom falters. They are rather extravagant in their support of him when he is entrusted by his village with Ikemefuna, the child hostage given to Umofia in compensation for the murder of a woman from Umofia by the neighbouring village of Mbaino. With a stunning graciousness, the women take the lad under their wings without raising a finger. Even when there is good reason to question his judgement, as happens when he beats second wife Ojiugo for serving him a late meal, the wives' interest in helping Okonkwo to protect his public image always prevails. They not only do what is expected of them with enthusiasm and zest, but often they go beyond the call of duty in offering their love. In none of the major events where women are called upon to extend themselves do we find any of Okonkwo's wives wanting in the display of goodwill, integrity and dedication.

It is no surprise that the events exhibiting the most profoundly sustained expressions of tenderness, love, devotion and altruism in the traditional African polygamous household all involve women's communal work, be it cooking or painting, the application of the decorative arts, or dancing, all of which are areas where women exercise a clear dominance in the traditional Igbo culture. The extent to which this society depends on its womenfolk, especially in carrying out its ritual duties or organizing festivals, is therefore huge, and in this context three events particularly stand out: the occasion where the Umofia village is preparing for the New Yam Festival; the *uri*, otherwise known as the bride-offering ceremony (where Obierika's daughter Akueke is being given in marriage to Ibe, her suitor); and the scene of Okonkwo's farewell party for his Mbanta kinsmen.

We may begin with the New Yam Festival, a sort of thanksgiving ceremony in honour of *Ani*, 'the earth goddess and the ancestral spirits of the clan' responsible for fertility (26). Held 'every year before the harvest began', it is on this occasion that the yam is publicly recognized as the community's most important food crop, one standing for 'manliness' since 'he who could feed his family on yams from one harvest to another was a very great man indeed' (23). Naturally, during this ceremony a mood of festivity like no other graces the entire villages of Umofia, because nothing brings a man greater respect than yams, and 'Men and women, young and old, looked forward to the New Yam Festival because it began the season of plenty – the new year' (26). Yet, even though the New Yam Festival is without question one of the few exclusively male-affirming events in the community, women do more than just take an active part in making the event happen. It is the women's presence that adds nuance and colour to the ceremony which cannot conceivably take place without the sheer sense of spectacle they contribute, in addition to being far and away the heart and soul of the occasion.

The stellar performance of Okonkwo's wives during this event particularly helps to illuminate the sense of the importance attached to domesticity, giving a measure of the social, material and emotional investment that women make into the corporate life of their staunchly masculine society. Coming into their own, Okonkwo's wives show they can hold their ground with anyone and live in complete harmony with their husband's dreams and aspirations:

> The festival was now only three days away. Okonkwo's wives had scrubbed the walls and the huts with red earth until they reflected light. They had drawn patterns on them in white, yellow and dark green. They then set about painting themselves with cam wood and drawing beautiful black patterns on their stomachs and on their backs. The children were also decorated, especially their hair, which was shaved in beautiful patterns. The three women talked excitedly about the relations who had been invited, and the children revelled in the thought of being spoilt by these visitors from motherland. Ikemefuna was excited. The New Yam Festival seemed to him to be a much bigger event here than in his own village, a place which was already becoming remote and vague in his imagination. (27)

All present in this scene of women's communal work uniformly recognize one important fact: elegance, surface glamour, visual animation, and synergy set the enabling mood for festivity; that height and grandeur are the materials of a banquet. They are the conditions necessary for the release of the larger-than-life mood that a festival occasion aspires to attain in order to complete the emptying-out of individuals from their personal protective shells. That is why the female group steps up to the plate and helps with its multiple skills that men, by their calling and constitution, do not possess – cleaning, braiding, carrying out body and wall painting, as well as decoration. Of the attributes of the domestic setting within the closely knit traditional Igbo polygamous household that reveal themselves through women's communal work, notable are the ways in which women learn to function as a team in order to secure the public good, favouring collectivity and unity over narrowly set personal interests. Since success in the assigned mission depends on everyone doing her part, self-interest has to yield to the selfless desire to promote the tradition of which all are a part because each wife can see her personal aspirations wrapped up in the welfare of the community to which the public image of her husband too is tied. Applying the skills of the decorative arts becomes an essential social obligation that the women dispense not just because of the capacity of colours to connect in fixing a certain (positive or negative) image of society, but, more importantly, because along with that it is the constitutive act of spiritual devotion.

It is in a cheerful and rambunctious mood that the women of Okonkwo's household team up as they step up to cook. Indeed, showing so much dexterity and excitement, radiating such a high level of generosity and bubbling over with *joie de vivre* as if they were born to do this, they pool the children of the household into an effective kitchen team; thus Ekwefi and Ezinma prepare the hen; Nwoye's mother (Okonkwo's first wife) peels the yams; Ikemefuna, Nwoye, his two younger brothers and his sister Obiageli get the water.

> Ezinma went outside and brought some sticks from a huge bundle of firewood. She broke them into little pieces across the sole of her foot and began to build a fire, blowing it with her breath.
>
> 'You will blow your eyes out,' said Nwoye's mother, looking up from the yams she was peeling. 'Use the fan.' She stood up and pulled out the fan which was fastened into one of the rafters. As soon as she got up, the troublesome nanny-goat, which had been

dutifully eating yam peelings, dug her teeth into the real thing, scooped out two mouthfuls and fled from the hut to chew the cud in the goats' shed. Nwoye's mother swore at her and settled down again to her peeling. Ezinma's fire was now sending up thick clouds of smoke. She went on fanning it until it burst into flames. Nwoye's mother thanked her and she went back to her mother's hut. (30)

This is an especially accurate account of the typical atmosphere associated with women's communal work in the polygamous house-hold because it establishes the symbiotic roles of compliment and reproach as key components of instructional method related to the education of children, as well as the women's vital part in the trans-mission of culture.

To show that the women are more adept than the men in setting up the enabling moods for festival during the bride-offering cere-mony of Obierika's daughter Akueke, emphasis is particularly on the master plot of Igbo traditional life: an ideology of social regen-eration contingent upon involvement of women as key players in the game. The bride-giving ceremony is singularly critical to the contin-uation of family, the very source of life in the traditional Igbo setting, because bearing a child out of wedlock is not just rejected but tabooed. That is why public acknowledgement of the impor-tance accorded to wifehood by honouring the bride's mother implies recognition of the importance attached to wifehood by honouring motherhood, a crucial aspect of a broader practice by which the male suitor is required to formally and finally ratify his decision to commit to and invest in the life-long dual institutions of wifehood and motherhood. For this reason, the bride's 'suitor (having already paid the greater part of her bride-price) would bring palm-wine not only to her parents and immediate relatives but to the wide and extensive group of kinsmen called *umunna*' (77).

Yet, while the Igbos set great store by getting the entire commu-nity involved in the bride-giving ceremony – because marriage for them is a communal affair, an event that binds not only two individ-uals but also whole communities together, and hence that depends for its survival as a corporate institution on the commitment of everyone – the bride-giving event is really 'a woman's ceremony' and so 'the central figures' are 'the bride and her mother' (77).[14] Hence, as Okonkwo's three wives lead other women in giving public recognition to this importance accorded to the bride-giving ceremony, as an occasion to pay tribute to marriage and motherhood as some of the most important aspects of society's cherished cultural capital, they show unusual largesse with their labour and substance:

> Okonkwo's family was astir like any other family in the neighbourhood. Nwoye's mother and Okonkwo's youngest wife were ready to set out for Obierika's compound with all their children . . . Nwoye's mother carried a basket of coco-yams, a cake of salt and smoked fish which she would present to Obierika's wife. Okonkwo's youngest wife, Ojiugo, also had a basket of plantains and coco-yams and a small pot of palm-wine. Their children carried pots of water.
>
> Ekwefi was tired and sleepy from the exhausting experiences of the previous night. It was not very long since they had returned . . .
>
> Ezinma was still sleeping when everyone else was astir, and Ekwefi asked Nwoye's mother and Ojiugo to explain to Obierika's wife that she would be late. She had got ready her basket of coco-yams and fish, but she must wait for Ezinma to wake. (77–8)

This passage indicates clearly that Achebe has a keen sensitivity to gender issues, and in *Things Fall Apart* he assigns the tender qualities to women who are the bloodline through which the life of their society flows. As indicated in the passage quoted above, the motive for action by the women emerges not only as a deep sense of social obligation but also as a genuine labour of love. The women of Okonkwo's household take their social duty so seriously, they will allow nothing to hinder it. But they give so wholeheartedly of themselves for the public good, despite the level of self-sacrifice this entails, not just because Igbo custom demands that in performing ritual roles personal comfort of neccessity becomes a secondary consideration. Okonkwo's wives give for their own enjoyment and satisfaction too; for them, giving is really a personal thing, a part of their very being; it is the justification for their very existence.[15]

A major theme of the novel is that while the Igbos generally care very deeply about the quality of the devotion of love, affection appears to be a special priority for women to whom the tender instincts come more naturally than they do to the menfolk. Usually

the level of love interest is registered during the bride-giving ceremony by the quantity and quality of food and drinks served. The
pattern of role distribution, by which the responsibility for the provision of the food rests squarely upon the wife-givers while the duty
of supplying drinks for the banquet devolves upon the wife-takers,
allows the two parties to strive aggressively to outdo each other.
When interest is evenly balanced, as is the case shown at the event in
Obierika's residence, neither the wife-givers nor the wife-takers
swerving in the gesture of support that they are seen to be offering,
the result is explosive. Thus, Obierika's compound becomes 'as busy
as an ant-hill. Temporary cooking tripods were erected on every
available space by bringing together three blocks of sun-dried earth
and making a fire in their midst' (78–9). The rippling effect of the
women's obsessive behaviour on the men is described as follows:

> Cooking pots went up and down the tripods, and foo-foo was
> pounded in a hundred wooden mortars. Some of the women
> cooked the yams and the cassava, and others prepared the vege-
> table soup. Young men pounded the foo-foo or split firewood.
> The children made endless trips to the stream.
>
> Three young men helped Obierika to slaughter the two goats
> with which the soup was made. They were very fat goats, but the
> fattest of all was tethered to a peg near the wall of the compound.
> It was as big as a small cow. Obierika had sent one of his relatives
> all the way to Umuike to buy that goat. It was the one he would
> present alive to his in-laws. (79)

This passage offers poignant images of behaviour exemplary of the
marriage institution: in a contest conducted with good humour, each
party is striving to out-give the other: giving its very best, with love
more than anything else and joyous abandon; not frugally but liber-
ally. Yet, when reading closely, the force of gender makes it impossible not to see that the motives for the behaviour of the men and the
women are entirely different. Women tend to give their very best
because they believe that true love is outward-looking, not inward-
looking. The men appear to catch the women's spirit quickly, but
only up to a point because their actions are more calculated. This is
seen in the way that Obierika raises the stakes, offering his prospec-
tive in-laws 'the fattest of all' the goats he could find.

It is the character of Obierika who offers Achebe the opportunity to explore the differences between altruistic action by the women and that by the men, which is almost always self-interested. When Obierika gives of his best, it is as though he recognizes that difficult in-laws are notorious for being behind many a failed marriage and he wants to lay a solid groundwork for a future good relationship through actions that suggest deep love and generosity. Capitalizing upon the spirit embodied in the economy of marriage gift-exchange that one good turn deserves another is a way for him to secure the future of his daughter's anticipated marriage.

Whatever the motive, however, the end always justifies the means when it comes to the security of marriage, something the Igbos generally see as a wise investment. That is why an assurance of the preservation of the institution of marriage invariably overrides any focus on difference or gender biases in the economy of the competitive gift-exchange. Thus, though the contest pattern of the gift-exchange in the bride-giving ceremony harks back powerfully to the pattern of the wrestling match in the novel's opening pages, the Igbos are not confused about the differences. They are aware that unlike the wrestling bout, at which victory is won by egocentrism or self-interest, the engine of performance in marriage is fired by a love interest expressed in acts that are indicative of generosity toward the other partner. So ultimately actions speak louder than thoughts, and generosity is evidence that love gives because it is more concerened with the other person than it is concerned with the self.[16]

The Igbos seek the involvement of the entire community as one body – wife-givers and wife-takers as well as others; women, children and adults – acting in unison to make marriage work because it is implied that the goodwill of everyone is required, and all are duty-bound, to make marriage work, since everyone's interest is at stake when it comes to this primary unit of society – the nuclear family – for which union between man and woman is the main foundation. If the bride-giving ceremony offers a touchstone for public celebration – a site where marriage is acknowledged as not only a personal but also a shared experience – it is because marriage is an institution that binds entire communities together, contrary to the impression that it is merely 'a union of two family groups' (Okafor, 2002: 121).

The epitome of the love affair that attends women's communal endeavour in the traditional Igbo polygamous households occurs at the farewell feast thrown by Okonkwo for his mother's people to end his exile. On that occasion, the exemplary sharing, delegation of duty, and sisterhood without rancour that women exhibit during communal labour find their fullest expression:

> Ekwefi still had some cassava left on her farm from the previous year. Neither of the other wives had. It was not that they had been lazy, but that they had many children to feed. It was therefore understood that Ekwefi would provide cassava for the feast. Nwoye's mother and Ojiugo would provide the other things like smoked fish, palm oil and pepper for the soup. Okonkwo would take care of meat and yams. (116)

Here it can be seen that, as the women of Okonkwo's household work together like a well-oiled machine, everything falls into place: roles are accepted and played out with good humour by everyone, enabling the smooth take-off of the function. The reader is reminded that the purpose of the feast itself is to cement commonality among 'all the descendants of Okolo who had lived about two hundred years before' (116). When Uchendu, 'the oldest member of this extensive family', prays, he confirms this ideal of human connectedness:

> The kola nut was given to him to break, and he prayed to the ancestors. He asked them for health and children. 'We do not ask for wealth because he that has health and children will also have wealth. We do not pray to have more money but to have more kinsmen. We are better than animals because we have kinsmen. An animal rubs its aching flank against a tree, a man asks his kinsmen to scratch him.' He prayed especially for Okonkwo and his family. He then broke the kola nut and threw one of the lobes on the ground for the ancestors. (117)

An interesting piece of Igbo traditional ritual rhetoric, Uchendu's prayer contains a great deal that draws attention to the humanistic values of the Igbos. In their economy of values, relationship and good health are society's most important treasures, not material goods which always come second; a marked contrast with Okonkwo's materialistic obsessions over which anyone with a temperate judgement should be rightly concerned. That's why, when offering his closing remarks, Uchendu thanks Okonkwo for giving them a lavish feast that is satisfying as well as spectacular and then gives his nephew a gentle reprimand, reiterating even further the primacy of human community in the Igbo people's scale of values; the prime reason that the progressive drive toward excessive individualism which is rearing its ugly head in their midst is quite disturbing.

The narrative makes clear that the Igbos make relationship their core value because they consider unity a people's greatest strength. Group participation is an expression of empathetic understanding required not only to cement solidarity among a people but also to maximize gratification and interchange of emotions to cement solidarity but to maximize gratification and interchange of emotions among a people. Indeed, the whole of the occasion of public commemoration is a dramatization of the supremacy of community, which is also the struggle for the banishment of egocentrism. Thus, like Uchendu, another elder also expresses the conviction that human bonds are the most important of life's countless gifts. Friendship is important to this elder, not necessarily because the individual alone is insufficient but because when individual fixation gives way to the more inclusive and also more open companionship, it releases the full force of revelry: 'A man who calls his kinsmen to a feast does not do so to save them from starving. They all have food in their homes' (118). He puts it another way:

'When we come together in the moonlit village ground it is not because of the moon. Every man can see it in his own compound. We come together because it is good for kinsmen to do so. You may ask why I am saying all this. I say it because I fear for the younger generation, for you people.' He waved his arm where most of the young men sat. 'As for me, I have only a short while to live, and so have Uchendu and Unachukwu and Emefo. But I fear for you young people because you do not understand how strong is the bond of kinship. You do not know what it is to speak with one voice. And what is the result? An abominable religion has settled among you. A man can now leave his father and his brothers. He can curse the gods of his fathers and his ancestors, like a hunter's dog that suddenly goes mad and turns on his master. I fear for you; I fear for the clan.' (118)

The traditional Igbo society's main concern is to stabilize friendship; it erects a defensive wall against alienation because tradition venerates connection, understanding and unity. That is why the increasing movement toward excessive individualism represents a grave deformation of that native Igbo way of life. The Igbo way of valorizing life is through endowing people with an ultimate sense of worth. The magic of unity, of people coming together as one body, is cooperation whereby they share each other's joys and burdens, and extend love and nourishment to one another. The anonymous elder attributes the collapse of things in contemporary times to aggressive individualism, the root cause of disunity; the sense of the falling apart of things inscribed in the title of the novel.

The vision of horror that presents itself to that anonymous elder, captured in the image of the hunter's dog, conveys the sense of the madness and irrationality and chaos of things unleashed by the dissolution of the old order, returning us full circle to one startling reality: On the surface this world, feared to be on the verge of imminent doom (or upside down), appears merely to belong to men (witness the unnamed speaker's exclusive references to 'he', 'kinsmen', 'men' and 'his father and his brothers'). Nevertheless, despite this gender bias, women play a bigger role than is stated. All through his speech this elder refuses to acknowledge the women's conspicuous presence but, by standing firmly behind their man, Okonkwo's wives (just like the other women at the function) prove it's not simply that women are pivotal to all of the refreshing and feasting – though there is no doubt it is their cooking which guarantees that everyone in attendance gets fed and refreshed. More importantly, women are visibly the prime agency that ensures the transformation of society's quest for ritual purification through social accommodation. Through their work, the women play a spiritual role which helps to ease Okonkwo's transition from a deeply troubled exile in Mbanta into what all believe will be a triumphant return to his Umofia homeland after what he himself calls 'seven wasted and weary years' (115). The vibrations created by the enchanting mood of the occasion make the connections between the human world and the mythical world of the gods and the goddess in the hills and the caves.[17]

Esther Y. Smith observes the dominance of 'images of women in narratives dealing with traditional African society, including the jealous co-wives, the barren women, the mothers hoping for sons, and the heroines whose extraordinary abilities lift them to positions of leadership' (1986: 30). It is remarkable to notice that, because Achebe's narrative does not idealize women, in *Things Fall Apart* there is none of this type of assigning to women the stereotypic images that permeate fiction about traditional African society. As indicated in *Things Fall Apart*, things are more complex than that:

the African women who are represented by Okonkwo's wives, the only women seen at close range and so logically drawn to any degree of detail in their individuality, are human, hence they have feelings like everyone else – feelings such as anger, anxiety, affection, ambition, fear, hopefulness, disappointment, exhilaration, sadness and joy – and they combine many statuses, major and ancillary. Thus, in addition to being daughters and wives and mothers, it is indicated that Igbo women can be priestesses like Chielo, the priestess of Agbala who boldly dominates everyone and everything including men and other women as well as nature – the hills and the caves and 'the outer silence of the night' (70), whenever the spirit of possession takes hold of her; and some are farmers (as Okonkwo's wives are); and they can fall sick like other people (as do Ezinma and Ekwefi). The complex lives of Okonkwo's wives and Chielo particularly indicate that Igbo women do not consider any of their duties to be casual ones, or their multiple roles to be conflicting.[18]

But, in return for all their loyalty, obedience and support, what do Okonkwo's wives, on behalf of their fellow womenfolk, receive from him? And what kind of father does he show himself to be? He rules his household like a tyrant, 'bullying his wives, intimidating his son and ill-treating the young Ikemefuna' (Palmer 1972: 54). Out of anger, he acts in contravention of tradition by beating his youngest wife Ojiugo during the Week of Peace. His misdemeanour is described by Ani, the goddess of the Earth, as an 'evil' that 'can ruin the whole clan' (22). Then he repeats the same mistake by shooting at another wife, Ekwefi, for cutting the leaves of a banana tree during the New Yam Festival, and thus nearly becomes a wife murderer, leaving readers to wonder what to make of the fact that, while cutting the leaves of a banana tree may appear insensitive, Igbo women are no strangers to the traditional use of banana leaves for cooking.

THE INTERSECTION OF FAMILY LIFE AND PUBLIC DUTY

All the textual evidence points to the liminality of Okonkwo's existence, to the fact that he is always full of surprises regarding the extremity to which he can push his actions, evidence of the deadly imbalance in his personality. As Paula Berggren rightly observes, while Okonkwo 'stammers under strong emotion and has recourse to his fists; he is arrogant and even a bully, yet he has an unadmitted tender side that appears in his relationship to his wife Ekwefi, his caring for Ezinma during her fever, and his attachment to Ikemefuna, whose death shatters him for days' (1997: 495). It has to be pointed out that the full effect of all these situations of fleeting moments of imperfectly suppressed affection alternating with unexpected moments of incivility and cruelty is disastrous for his family because it negates clear and consistent patterns of behaviour.

A consequence of the arbitrariness and inconsistency of uses of rules and procedures to deal with conduct that is out of line is that it makes Okonkwo become unable to create a positive household climate that rewards appropriate behaviour. This causes his family no small amount of confusion. Okonkwo's wives and children are constantly on edge, living in an atmosphere in which they do not know what to expect next. It is hardly surprising, given this unpredictability, rashness and poor home-management skills, that many of the family members become rebellious.

Nwoye is the starkest victim of all of this. Okonkwo's inability to challenge Nwoye to live according to his prescribed pattern of conduct particularly raises the issue of how a parent's good intentions can go completely awry if not backed by a coherent, well-thought-out, and systematically implemented action plan. The root cause, without question, of Okonkwo's fractured relationship with Nwoye is their diametrically divergent outlook. Okonkwo wants to bring Nwoye up, as Emmanuel Obiechina puts it nicely, 'in the warrior tradition by telling him "masculine stories of violence and bloodshed," while Nwoye prefers "the stories that his mother used to tell," which include the cosmic myth of the primeval quarrel of Earth and Sky' (1993: 128). It doesn't take a lot of effort to see the problem of a struggle to control the household space in the relationship between Okonkwo and Nwoye. But the matter of the disconnection between Nwoye and Okonkwo goes well beyond the fight over power. Important an element as Oedipal rivalry evidently is as a contributory factor in the conflict, more important is a decided lack of effective communication between father and son, for while it is obvious that Okonkwo has good intentions and evidently loves Nwoye dearly, it is also clear that he never once lets Nwoye know this. Instead, all Nwoye ever feels is the cold effect of his father's stern disciplinary hand.

One senses that all of the disciplinary action that Okonkwo directs at Nwoye stems out of the temper of a habitual worrywart with a tremendous capacity for love. For instance, correcting Nwoye harshly for not understanding 'the difficult art of preparing seed-yams' (23) is the result of Okonkwo's being overtly anxious about the young man's slow response to instruction. Okonkwo sees a young man's future as exclusively wrapped up in manliness. For him, therefore, Nwoye's poor showing in sturdiness, the manner of real men, is very disappointing because it's almost as if disorderly succession is occurring and the grandfather's personality is being passed down to the grandson. In short, Okonkwo is apprehensive about Nwoye's future because he perceives clear signs that the boy might end up a failure like his grandfather Unoka.

True, common sense should have told Okonkwo that a compromise is possible. But, characteristically enough, he doesn't have the discernment to grasp the lesson that the keys to a parent not alienating his children are treating them with respect and constant dialogue. Yet if Okonkwo could realize it, he does not really have to look far to find an action plan, since it is shown up most emphatically in his own home by the peerlessness of his relationship with his favourite daughter Ezinma, although he erroneously holds Obierika's relationship with his son Maduka in greater esteem – thus giving himself a reason to become progressively more envious of his friend.

The lesson that Okonkwo could take from his matchless relationship with Ezinma is lost on him because of his over-determined drive to blot out everything outside the bounds of his ambition to raise a boy for purposes of succession. The alternative to persuasion is the persistent authoritarian method Okonkwo uses in parenting. The more his orders escalate into threats and intimidation, the more Nwoye continues to defy him. But what Okonkwo cannot anticipate is the resentment to which Nwoye's suspicion that he has something to do with Ikemefuna's cold-blooded murder gives vent. Nwoye's missing the spirit of his father's good intentions causes their already fractured relationship to snap entirely when he commits the ultimate defiant act of converting to Christianity.

Replete as Okonkwo's conduct is with many contradictions, it also raises concerns about his lack of real authority, if authority is conceived as the power to have everything submit to one without one's having to exert much effort. It is weird enough that Okonkwo should presume his son would spontaneously esteem his authority, whereas he himself has despised and rejected his own father. Even more weird is the indication that not even his relationship with Ezinma is as without a cloud of uncertainty as might be thought, since it is not

really the person of Ezinma he admires but the idea of who he con-
ceives her to be, the potential she represents – his idea of what she
could be were she to be a male child, an inverted image of a model
son. His not really loving her for who she is but rather for an unful-
filled aspiration thus calls into question the admiration he claims to
profess for her, since this attitude is in the final analysis more revealing of the size of his ego. Okonkwo's unrealized desire is to raise a
male child who is as lofty and reserved as himself. He sees these traits
in their undeveloped forms in Ezinma; this is the primary source of
their mutual attraction to each other.

Some critics believe that Okonkwo is not entirely lacking in delicacy;
Ikemefuna's death is ironically cited as an episode that helps bring the
tender aspect of Okonkwo's personality to light. The misunderstand-
ing here is the fact that Okonkwo's distress is not really out of sympathetic identification with the ill-fated lad. Rather, he is truly more
troubled by other matters. Primarily, it is having to mount a public
defence against the reproachful judgement of his friends and other
community leaders for his role in the boy's murder that upsets
Okonkwo. As he struggles within himself to deal with the persistent
unrest in his mind due to the lack of a diversionary activity in his household to take up his attention during that season of the year, he himself
says that it makes no sense for 'a man who has killed five men in battle
to fall to pieces because he has added a boy to their number' (45).

We should not gloss over the fact that if Ikemefuna's death causes
Okonkwo some uneasiness, his discomfort springs far less out of an
unselfish feeling for the boy's fate than from his egotism, his own
self-serving ends: the loss of what is unquestionably the positive
influence Ikemefuna in the three years of living in his family has
brought to bear on Nwoye to the extent that the boys 'no longer
spent the evenings in mother's hut while she cooked' (37). Indeed, so
pleased is Okonkwo with the changes he sees around them that he
begins to encourage 'the boys to sit with him in his *obi*', where he
tells them 'stories of the land – stories of violence and bloodshed'
(37). It is therefore not without reason that Ikemefuna's death
should assail Okonkwo with some sense of loss. The obsessive
impulses that precipitate the unrest in Okonkwo's mind after the
boy's death are not all that different from those emotions which drive
him out, in disregard of the advice of Ezeudu and Obierika, to
murder his foster-son in the first place: his own grotesque self-
absorption, egocentrism and self-interest.

When the execution squad sets out on its mission to exact fulfilment of the oracle's pronouncement, Okonkwo could have stayed
home. But, intent upon satisfying his ego-driven ambitions, he not
only wilfully joins it, but, curiously enough, takes it upon himself to
deliver the fatal blow that dismembers the boy in his final moments.
Okonkwo's main motivation is a grotesque desire to project and
protect his own image as a warrior:

> One of the men behind him cleared his throat. Ikemefuna looked
> back, and the man growled at him to go on and not stand looking
> back. The way he said it sent cold fear down Ikemefuna's back.
> His hands trembled vaguely on the black pot he carried. Why had
> Okonkwo withdrawn to the rear? Ikemefuna felt his legs melting
> under him. And he was afraid to look back.
>
> As the man who had cleared his throat drew up and raised his
> matchet, Okonkwo looked away. He heard the blow. The pot fell
> and broke in the sand. He heard Ikemefuna cry, 'My father, they
> have killed me!' as he ran towards him. Dazed with fear,
> Okonkwo drew his matchet and cut him down. He was afraid of
> being thought weak. (43)

Okonkwo is driven to kill to make people think he still has it all
together; so he takes a human life because he wants to look good.
But contrary to his thoughts, his execution of his own foster-child is
no heroic display, for it rather turns the stomach as a vile act of cow-
ardice. Although the gory incident is obviously too chilling, too
painful, too tragic to allow a dispassionate interpretation of its
motivation, it is not surprising that it has far-reaching repercu-
sions.[19]

For one thing, Okonkwo's action is not lightly forgiven by either
of the men, Obierika or Ezeudu, who warned him against it; neither
is it absolved by his son, Nwoye. With even more important ramifi-
cations, it is not pardoned by the gods and goddesses of the land,
who appear to exact an uncanny retribution for it. Indeed,
Ikemefuna's killing, as it turns out, becomes spilled blood that
causes more blood to be spilled: as Obierika predicted, 'the kind of
action for which the goddess wipes out whole families' (46). The
gods and goddesses, it seems, allow no one opportunity for repen-
tance. And so, not long after the event, Ezeudu, the first to bear news
of the gods' ruling for the murder, not only loses his own life but his

own son is accidentally killed at his funeral; and killed by none other than Okonkwo, whom Ezeudu had discouraged passionately from having anything to do with the ritual murder. Then, Okonkwo is himself subsequently forced into exile, where his career suffers one reversal after another.

EUROPEAN CONQUEST: TRANSGRESSION AND DISLOCATION, OR SALVATION AND REHABILITATION?

Critics do not agree on the value of creating a calibrated scale on which to situate the legacy of the European occupation. Some think it merely one milepost on the long trail of changes the ever-evolving Igbo society has undergone, and which it soon readily navigated by allowing its citizens to assimilate what they found useful and reject what they found offensive within the new culture. To others the process is known as European intervention, an ostensibly altruistic mission that brought many positive changes to Africa, such as leveling the playing field by creating equal opportunities for all through Western education. Only European rule, in the opinion of these observers, held out the promise of rescuing the souls of the lost through Christianity; alleviating poverty through the monetary economy; eradicating the embedded injustice of the traditional African society by doing away with the existing social stratifications tied up with caste or class structures like the *osu* among the Igbos, the murder of twin babies, and generally bringing civilization to the benighted continent through the construction of good roads and the delivery of good healthcare measured by the provision of hospitals and clinics and modern medicine.[20]

Still others prefer the terminology of 'European takeover' as a more appropriate vocabulary for capturing the sense of the dramatic transformation caused by the imposition of European rule on Africa and the fundamental changes it forced upon the people both in the public sphere and in the private world upon which it impinged. These commentators refer to the collapse of the Igbo way of life and blame it on the burden of irreconcilable alien ideas and practices that starkly confound the natives. Since it's not as if Africans had any choice in the matter, the changes brought by the European presence are bitterly decried as the outcome of an unjust act of transgression. This is the position taken by Obierika in a conversation with Okonkwo not long after his return from exile:

'Does the white man understand our custom about land?'

'How can he when he does not even speak our tongue? But he says that our customs are bad; and our own brothers who have taken up his religion also say that our customs are bad. How do you think we can fight when our own brothers have turned against us? The white man is very clever. He came quietly and peaceably with his religion. We were amused at his foolishness and allowed him to stay. Now he has won our brothers, and our clan can no longer act as one. He has put a knife on the things that held us together and we have fallen apart.' (124–5)

The importance of unity and of other inherited values and norms of behaviour to the traditional Igbo society is here adumbrated in Obierika's lament about the confusion unleashed by the introduction of a new way of life. Whether carried out by quiet, peaceable means (in places like Umofia) or by violent military methods (as elsewhere, in places like Abame), pacification has an identical result in displacing the old order in Africa and causing bitter division and disorder among a people who once were united by a common identity. Therefore, in the view of some commentators, by failing to rally support effectively to ward it off, Okonkwo's role is symbolic of the local leadership's implication in the triumph of the British occupation of Igboland.

It is important to bear in mind the remark made by David Carroll in his influential study of Achebe. Arguing with his characteristic flair, he describes *Things Fall Apart*'s greatest contribution to world literature as residing in the composite image it provides of a tribal society working quite vibrantly as a living organ. Carroll surmises that critics who read this work with the usual expectations of the conventional novel will miss its central focus. He proposes that in *Things Fall Apart* Achebe did not simply replicate European fiction but added to the existing corpus in a significantly original way, to the extent that there is a surprising element to his creativity which lies in the presentation of a vivid communal consciousness. In the traditional novel the reader is 'nurtured on the attenuated diet of individual self-consciousness and introspection', but in *Things Fall Apart* 'the modulation from the communal life of the village to the individual consciousness and back again is unexpectedly powerful' (1990: 32–5).[21]

Carroll's study is itself a rare achievement; at once *explication de texte*, close reading, an exercise in value-making or evaluation and cultural studies, whose insightfulness makes it essential reading for all who wish to understand the craft of Achebe's fiction. In making a special claim for *Things Fall Apart*'s significance, he examines several passages in great detail. These include the arrival of the *egwugwu* or the ancestral spirits to settle a marriage dispute, the movement of the seasons marked by the arrival of the locusts and of the harmattan, as well as the case of Okonkwo and his sons 'repairing the walls of their compound' (Carroll, 1990: 34). All of these events illustrate, Carroll concludes, how 'the subtle rhythms of village life condition the characters' response to the events of the novel' (35). A unique achievement of *Things Fall Apart* lies, therefore, in its depiction of 'a clan in the full vigour of its traditional way of life, un-perplexed by the present and without nostalgia for the past. Through its rituals the life of the community and the life of the individual are merged into significance and order. This is most apparent in the village meetings which, interspersed through the action, give the novel so much of its special character' (32). Such is *Things Fall Apart*'s departure from the tradition of European fiction, it calls for a readjustment of readerly sensibilities for its contribution fully to be grasped. With Achebe's novel,

No longer is individual introspection the fictional norm as in the European novels of the nineteenth and twentieth centuries. It now appears foreign and unnatural, so that when the narrator begins to delve into the single mind we anticipate with foreboding an unpleasant turn of events. The individual seems vulnerable in his solitude and introspection; it is with relief that we see him reabsorbed into the community. There, his doubts and fears can be exorcised publicly and ritualistically. This is the dimension of the novel to which previous fiction has not accustomed us – the direct translation of problems, moral, political, and religious, into public debate and action. (Carroll, 1990: 35)

It's the vibrancy of the Igbo culture on display that makes the conflict that threatens to break it down not only all the more dramatic but also disconcerting. Far from being the vision of disorder and darkness painted by Europe, this is a society running smoothly on its own system of law and justice, morality and religion; its own method of burying its dead, and of self-regeneration.

In the full force of the law brought to bear in restoring the bad marriage of Uzowulu and Mgbafo, for instance, readers find a clear exemplification of the sense not only of the sanctity in which the institution of marriage is held by this society but also its notions of law and justice. Because M. Keith Booker offers a neat summary of that episode in terms that can hardly be improved upon, he is worth quoting at length:

> In one of the book's key demonstrations of the workings of justice in Umofia, the village elders meet to adjudicate a martial dispute in which the woman Mgbafo has fled the household of her husband, Uzowulu, because he has repeatedly beaten her (sometimes severely) for nine years. The legal proceedings are restricted to males, and no women (including Mgbafo) are allowed inside the hut where they occur . . . In the proceedings, Uzowulu presents his case, asking that Mgbafo be ordered to return to him. Then, Mgbafo's brother argues that she should be allowed to remain with him and her other brothers apart from her abusive husband. The elders (some of whom seem to regard the case as too trivial to be worthy of their attention) order Uzowulu to offer a pot of wine to Mgbafo's brothers in restitution. They refuse even to cast blame on the abusive husband, though the latter occurs not so much because they regard him as blameless as because they they see their role as one of restoring the peace rather than casting blame (2003: 253–4).

The Igbo traditional legal approach is seemingly self-contradictory. It appears to refuse to draw a fine line, a sharp distinction, between right and wrong, good and evil. It then seeks to use both oppositions to achieve reconciliation, rapprochement, when in fact these two extremes would seem to be irreconcilable. The implication here is that the Igbo legal system shows a disinclination to bring into direct confrontation the rightness and wrongness of cases couples bring before it because it is society's greater priority to speed up the healing process than to declare the winner or loser in a marital tussle. That's why, ultimately, what the system recommends as the most effective antidote to marital discord is the attitude of burying the hatchet, though society in no way encourages married couples to bury their heads in the sand. If we consider that decline of family is the inevitable tragic consequence that will follow were the institution of marriage to be allowed to collapse, we can see the wisdom of the style of evasion employed in favour of preserving that sacred institution. Thus, whereas cases like those which lead to Okonkwo's banishment from Umofia give the impression that the Igbo society is unforgiving and pays every crime a pound of flesh for a pound of flesh, marriage appears exceptional.

In conclusion, it might be observed that a marvel of *Things Fall Apart* is therefore how a story about the male struggle for authority and respect as well as economic and political empowerment masks a more disturbing tale about a divided sense of self and how women achieve power and respect within a patriarchy. The story also imbeds a narrative of dispossession that alters the meaning of life for an entire group of people who find themselves in an increasingly dichotomous world that begins to disconnect them from many of their vital native beliefs, norms, linguistic habits, and rituals. The novel's narrative nexus lays much stress on this drama of the collective dislocation of a society which walked a path that was derailed, marked by discontinuity and arbitrary external control; but it also takes in the beginning stories of European conquest, a mission that fed on the presumption that Europe was called upon to bring enlightenment to a people who largely prove unappreciative of the gifts of modern civilization. Mainly because we witness a feast celebrating the pleasures of traditional communal life, the message that it is about to be destroyed completely comes with the ultimate stamp of irony.

DISCUSSION POINTS

1. Courtship and the making of marriage are among the most important aspects of the culture of the Igbos represented in this novel. Unlike the situation in many societies, formal ceremonial processes guide the path of courtship leading to marriage among the Igbos. Trace this path as outlined in the novel (pp. 49–52; 76–82). Then analyse what the details tell us about Igbo gender ideas of beauty and morality, aesthetics and conduct.

2. The story has an obsession with what is involved in the Igbo concept of manhood or heroism. Carefully explain what it means to be a man or a hero in this culture. As a corollary, the story gives detailed coverage to the idea and praxis of womanhood. Conduct a parallel study of the concept of womanhood in the Igbo culture.

3. The issue of father–son rivalry depicted, for example, in James

Joyce's *Finnegan's Wake*, is featured in *Things Fall Apart* but presented from a different perspective. Write a detailed study of the Okonkwo–Nwoye split.

4. The story is quite emphatic about the role submission to authority plays in the maintenance of family bonds and fraternal ties among the Igbos. How is the culture defined by this practice?
5. This story has a major focus on the role the missionaries played in the destruction of the old order in Igboland. Use the diametrically opposed characters of evangelists Brown and Smith to clarify some of the complications of proselytization (pp. 130–5).
6. 'The white man is very clever. He came quietly and peaceably with his religion. We were amused at his foolishness and allowed him to stay. Now he has won our brothers, and our clan can no longer act like one. He has put a knife on the things that held us togther and we have fallen apart' (pp. 124–5). Use this statement as a starting point for an elaboration of the argument alleging the complicity of Igbos in their own domination.

QUESTIONS AND SUGGESTIONS FOR FURTHER STUDY

1. What do you make of the images of children in communal play activities? What do they say about the ability to work in common on the one hand and self-sufficiency or the inability to work with others on the other?
2. Why does Obierika succeed in bringing up Maduka as a son who has much in common with him while Okonkwo fails to attain similar results with Nwoye?
3. What does Nwoye resent the most about his father? What does he find the most appealing about Christianity by contrast?
4. What aspects of Maduka's character does Okonkwo admire the most and regret not seeing in his own son Nwoye?
5. Of the characters of Okonkwo and Unoka, which is the more attactive?
6. What do the Igbos think of themselves and of other people, including both their immediate neighbours and their distant ones, the Europeans?
7. Indicate the instances where Okonkwo behaves like a snob.
8. List the various episodes in the story woven around conflict and establish the symbolic links between them.

9. Attack or defend the conclusion that the killing of twins and the treatment of *osus* manifest clear aspects of the cruelty embedded in traditional Igbo culture.
10. What do the horrors experienced by Ikemefuna at the liminal space of death, first at the threat and then at the stark reality of death, at the moment of his transition between life and death, reveal about the culture of terror?

CHAPTER 4

CRITICAL RECEPTION, INTERPRETATION AND AFTERLIFE (ADAPTATION AND INFLUENCE)

It is remarkable how much of the mass of attention devoted to Achebe's work as a creative writer (novelist, short-story stylist, poet, and writer of children's books) that *Things Fall Apart* has garnered. Published criticism of *Things Fall Apart* - in its various, complex, critical methods, in its various incarnations, from its most elementary to its most sophisticated forms – traverses several paths. These range from the anthropological method to reader response or impressionism, historical/biographical, psychological, legal, moral/ philosophical, semiotic/stylistic/linguistic and generic approaches, some of which utilize an eclectic combination of several methods of reading, while others are situated within the fine lines of recognizable paradigms.

Anthropology, the mode with which the interpretation of African literature first began, as signalled by the earliest Western responses to Amos Tutuola's *The Palm-Wine Drinkard* (1952), also inaugurated the extended study of Achebe's novels. This began with the appearance of what have now become well-known and widely quoted studies such as Austin Shelton's 'The Offended *Chi* in Achebe's Novels' (1964) and 'The "Palm-Oil" of Language: Proverbs in Chinua Achebe's Novels' (1969); Bernth Lindfors' 'The Palm Oil with which Achebe's Words are Eaten' (1968); Ernest Emenyonu's 'Ezeulu: The Night Mask Caught Abroad by Day' (1971); Donatus Nwoga's 'The "Chi", Individualism and Igbo Religion' (1971); Lloyd Brown's 'Cultural Norms and Modes of Perception' (1972); Tunji Adebayo's 'The Past and the Present in Chinua Achebe's Novels' (1974) as well as J. Z. Kronenfeld's 'The "Communalistic" African and the "Individualistic" Westerner' (1975), among others.

What all these pioneering studies in the anthropological method have in common is the stress they place upon how Achebe's works reveal their unique background. If anthropology has been a particularly good fit for Achebe study, it is because of the strong ethnic roots of his writing. These early explorations have provided reference points for other later studies too numerous to list here, as testified by the excellent works that have inundated the field, some of which are collected in the volumes *Critical Perspectives on Chinua Achebe* (1979), edited by C. L. Innes and Bernth Lindfors; *Understanding Things Fall Apart: Selected Essays and Criticism* (1998), edited by Solomon Iyasere; *Chinua Achebe's Things Fall Apart: Modern Critical Interpretations* (2002), edited by Harold Bloom; and *Chinua Achebe's Things Fall Apart: A Casebook* (2003), edited by Isidore Okpewho.

By straddling both the anthropological and formalistic approaches, the publication in 1970 of David Carroll's comprehensive book *Chinua Achebe* (revised 1980 and 1990) made available for the first time for Achebe studies the possibilities of extended critical elaboration and analysis of Achebe's creative works (novels, short stories, and poems) in reference to both their informing Igbo expressive idiom and locale and their European-language tradition. It was not until ten years later, however, when Robert Wren published *Achebe's World* (1980), followed in quick succession by Emmanuel Okoye's book *The Traditional Religion and Its Encounter with Christianity in Chinua Achebe's Novels* (1987) and Kalu Ogbaa's *Gods, Oracles and Divination* (1992), that the traditional outlines of the anthropological enterprise were to be expanded and given a new energy by authors who expertly weave biography with history in such a way as to give anthropological criticism a new force and direction.

If pursued as an end in itself, the anthropological approach easily renders its practitioner liable to the error of mislocating the value of an art object largely in its context of expression. Acutely aware of this limitation of their working tool, the overwhelming majority of anthropological Achebe scholars have tended to apply their craft with tact by using details of his background mainly to explore the power of his narrative. The best uses of anthropological concerns therefore anchor Achebe's works within the specificity of their milieu, offering a compelling portrait of both the culture and its bearing on the work's subject of exploration, underlining the links between the creative temper and its context of expression. In the years that scholars were effecting a decisive reversal of anthropological approaches to the reading of Achebe's novels, however, substantial evidence had been gathered to point toward anthropology's insufficiency as a mode for exclusively bringing an adequate understanding to the full contours of the literary value of Achebe's works.

Although an anthropological approach was sustained throughout most Achebe criticism of the 1960s and 70s, the shift to the dominant formalistic mode of reading of the 80s had already been prefigured by the 1964 publication of Eldred D. Jones's laconic study 'Language and Theme in *Things Fall Apart*', an essay that was followed closely by Abiola Irele's study 'The Tragic Conflict in Chinua Achebe's novels' (1965), both of which marked great watershed moments in the attempt to bring new tools of analysis to bear on the critical reading of Achebe's works. Ironically, formalism as a critical response to Achebe was dormant throughout most of the 60s and 70s.

It was not until the publications of C. L. Innes' *Chinua Achebe* (1990) and Simon Gikandi's *Reading Chinua Achebe* (1991) that anthropology as an approach to Achebe's work became fully supplanted by formalism. Innes' and Gikandi's books, representing the most detailed and robust attempts to break with anthropolgy as the central mode for reading Achebe's works, bring into full flowering the fruits of trends whose threads line such other works that followed on the heels of Jones and Irele as Donald Weinstock and Cathy Ramadan's 'Symbolic Structure in *Things Fall Apart*' (1969); Solomon Iyasere's 'Narrative Techniques in *Things Fall Apart*' (1974); Bu-Buakei Jabi's 'Fire and Transition in *Things Fall Apart*' (1975); Emmanuel Ngara's 1982 book *Stylistic Criticism and the African Novel*; and Angela Smith's 'The Mouth with which to tell of their Suffering: The Role of the Narrator and Reader in Achebe's *Things Fall Apart*' (1988).

Formalistic Achebe criticism emerged, and became stabilized, not through a deliberate campaign but as part of a stirring critique by its proponents of the then reigning anthropological approaches. Yet the chief idea underpinning formalism as a mode of reading is a revolutionary idea: that Achebe is a conscious craftsman whose works are better served by greater attention being paid to their literary rather than to their non-literary content. Thus, for Gikandi, the guiding notion is that in writing his novels Achebe had 'a self-conscious desire to produce African literature which will use the language of the hegemonic culture to express the desire for cultural liberation' (1991b: 25). Gikandi is therefore convinced that the techniques that could usefully be employed to explicate Achebe's works can be found only within post-structuralist theories which have been successfully applied to the works of metropolitan English writers, of which he believes Achebe's novels to be derivative.

This is a conviction implicitly shared, even if not officially voiced, by many formalists. It is elaborated, for instance, in C. L. Innes' *Chinua Achebe* (1990), which sets out to demonstrate that Achebe's writings – though inevitably about African subjects – are yet deeply embedded, formalistically, within the Western tradition. Specifically, among the main points put forward by Innes' study is that Joyce Cary's *Mister Johnson* is central to the form and design of Achebe's first two novels (12) and that claims (made by Charles Nnolim for *Arrow of God*) that Achebe derives the primary inspiration for his novels from his indigeneous Igbo sources are wrong in their entirety.

With their emphases upon theoretically nuanced close readings, the unique contributions made by formalistic Achebe studies by the likes of Gikandi and Innes move beyond pioneering efforts such as those by G. D. Killam (1969), in erasing stereotypes of formalism as merely plot summarizing peppered occasionally with moralizing commentary. In the absence of much that other critics can add to the formulations generated in the footsteps of the studies by Innes and Gikandi, Achebe formalist scholarship appears to have lost its steam. Reflecting the impression that formalist Achebe study has quickly burned out its flames are the extended studies by Emmanuel Edame Egar (*The Rhetorical Implications of Chinua Achebe's Things Fall Apart*, 2000) and by Chinwe Christiana Okechukwu (*Achebe the Orator*, 2001), in both of which the focus is surprisingly on showing how Achebe's rhetoric resembles Greek oratory rather than the nuances of oral Igbo noetic.

Predominating in Achebe scholarship in the wake of formalism's apparent eclipse, from about the mid-90s to date, has been an extensive turn to thematic criticism combining a pastiche of critical approaches that includes impressionism, reader response, post-colonial temper, psychoanalysis and cultural studies, sprinkled with doses of moralistic commentary and philosophical content analysis. The books by Ojinmah (1991), Muoneke (1994), Simola (1995), and Ogede (2001) are representative of this trend. What Umelo Ojinmah sets out to do in his *Chinua Achebe: New Perspectives*, for example, is to examine the motif of power as an explanatory trope in Achebe's novels, and he draws substantial support for his conclusions from Achebe's own socio-political commentary, arguing passionately in the introductory sections of his study that no other issue is as central to the logic of Achebe's fiction as his interest in the ways in which responsibility or power is handled, before each of the five succeeding chapters of his book then offers readings that illustrate the ways in which various key characters have enabled or hindered Achebe's exploration of the different facets of the development in his fiction of the critic's chosen topic of discussion.

For his part, Romanus Okey Muoneke in *Art, Rebellion and Redemption* focuses on the image of European missionaries in the proselytization of Igboland as depicted in fiction by Achebe, and reports in his findings that they 'included people who exhibited exemplary qualities' and not only helped in 'the growth' of the new faith but also built schools and hospitals (1994: 110), while Raisa Simola, who invites readers to see the value of the canon of Achebe's writings – short fiction, novels, essays, juvenile literature, and poetry – through both their specific Igbo ethnic world-view and that of a mutative postcolonial Africa in general, mostly discusses the major characters and narrators of Achebe's fiction as masks of his own personality. For Simola, *Things Fall Apart*'s main interest is to display the rhythm of the rural life of the Igbos and their world-view which came into conflict with the contradictory imposed European culture. Ogede presents colonialism as the main event that both inspired and provided the subject for all Achebe's writing, including *Things Fall Apart*, which he sees as being ideologically limited by its informing vision, particularly its reliance on the plot of Greek tragedy.

Like African literature generally, and even the literary practice in the traditional fields of English and American literature also, feminism is a latecomer to Achebe criticism. In the years since its emergence, however, feminist Achebe criticism has sprinted along quite briskly. Much of the groundwork for this type of interpretation in the general field of African literature was first laid out in *Ngambika: Studies of Women in African Literature* (Davies and Graves, eds, 1986). Although Achebe is briefly acknowledged there, it wasn't until the early 1990s that feminist Achebe criticism really took off with the impetus provided by Rhonda Cobham's 'Problems of gender and history in the teaching of *Things Fall Apart*' (1990), in which a gendered reading leads to the accusation that Achebe's presentation reinforces dominant male Christian views of traditional Igbo society and the suggestion that male chauvinism is the prime reason the novel has always appealed to mainstream critics.

Several scholars have since taken up Rhonda Cobham's battle cry for the incorporation of the female viewpoint into the literary reading of *Things Fall Apart*, including Biodun Jeyifo (1993), who gave us a trenchant Marxist-inspired study; Florence Stratton (1994), who approached the field from a psychoanalytic viewpoint; as well as Chioma Opara (1998), Obioma Nnaemeka (1998), and Catherine Bicknell (1998), who all place emphasis on the formal properties; and also Kwadwo Osei-Nyame (1999), whose study poignantly reflects Bakhtinian-inflected interests. All this diversity is as it should be given that feminism is, as R. B. Kershner has correctly noted, 'of course not merely a literary approach but a worldwide social movement and philosophy, or group of philosophies' which has 'altered not only the accepted canon of literary works we study and the kinds of interpretation we bring to bear on them, but the very language we all speak and the laws and customs that formalize our cultural consensus' (1997: 93).

One thing will have to be admitted: the many ways in which critics have shown, and continue to show, that Achebe's works can be read, and the great warmth of affection readers have radiated, and continue to radiate, toward him – both as an author and as a person – all indicate the central position Achebe has come to occupy in the hearts of his readers worldwide. In more than four decades of critical attention, Achebe has not simply been transformed into an international celebrity, as some critics would have it, but made a citizen of the world who has charmed people of all nationalities because they can all claim his story as their own. Put another way, Achebe is no longer simply a local author, a patron of sacred values from the past held up for custodianship for his ethnic group; no longer a national figure defending his country against foreign detractors. From the critics' accolades and the remarkable analyses showing the extraordinary power of his imagination, it is easy to see that, as an author able to draw his story – the most primitive of art forms – into the maelstrom of modernity, Achebe has been destined from the start not only for stardom but also for eternal enshrinement as a monumental aspect of our human literary history. For his many excellent contributions to the expanding canon of world literature and culture, our debts to Chinua Achebe are therefore immense, for he has truly made it such an exciting time for us to be among the living.

Although he was by no means the first African author to write a literature of self-understanding, Achebe's works have headed the roster of those that provided, and continue to provide, a model for other African writers interested in the effort to bring history and fiction together in an attempt to document the culture clash that arose from Africa's contact with Europe. Judging by the evaluations of his critics, Achebe's leadership derives from the unique energy and style of cultural retrieval to which he committed himself, an exploration whose special chemistry issues from a splendid mode of appropriation of African and European narrative techniques. Through the mastery of a distinctly original expressive power, Achebe stretches the conventionalized mode of construction in the English language to its very limits without impeding communication or destroying the rules of English grammar.

It is a remarkable quality of *Things Fall Apart* that it has spawned many imitations, not only by other writers of Achebe's own generation but also from the subsequent ones, and even Achebe himself has repeatedly had recourse to it as he has widened the scope of his fictional exploration to include other aspects of colonization. *Things Fall Apart*'s widespread impact is owed without a doubt to the innovations in literary uses of the techniques of orality it inaugurated. The oral tradition is a force to which a writer can repeatedly return because it seems a resource that is inexhaustible. A self-renewing tool from which much can be picked up to bring writing to life, it answers to all situations. No wonder that Achebe himself has repeatedly drawn from the pool of orality, and has in turn inspired many, including Elechi Amadi, Buchi Emecheta, John Munuonye, Onuora Nzekwu, Adaora Ulasi and Flora Nwapa – all of whom are concerned with cultural rehabilitaion – to gravitate toward his example. But in as much as Achebe has inspired an entire genre of fiction by a group of writers of his own Igbo ethnic origin, it is also true that his influence transcends his local settings, radiating as it has done to all corners of Africa and perhaps even beyond.

Indeed, the list of writers who acknowledge their debts to Achebe one way or another has widened so vastly as to include quite unlikely figures, such as Ngugi wa Thiong'o, Dambudzo Marechera and Ben Okri – artists who are unlikely candidates for the subject of exploring links with Achebe, not only because of the high degree of experimentation in their works but also because their works are so different on the surface that at first sight it appears unlikely readers can find any links between them. Because these links go beyond the issue of sharing common themes like ancestor worship, cultural nationalism, socio-political disillusionment, to issues relating to uses of similar linguistic modes, the situation has further complicated the protean difficulty of mapping literary alliance, influence, debt or borrowing, or even plain plagiarism or stolen words.

For example, Ngugi's *The River Between* (1965) is a remarkable variation of *Things Fall Apart*, in much the same way as his *A Grain of Wheat* (1967) offers a classical radical revision of Achebe's *Arrow of God*, and Achebe's *Things Fall Apart* in an obverse way is a rewriting of the focus of Cyprian Ekwensi's *People of the City* (1954). And so, although Sophocles' *Oedipus Rex* has been suggested as a possible model for *Things Fall Apart*, most notably by Michael Valdez Moses (1995), perhaps even more important is the matter of *Things Fall Apart*'s own imprint on other works, not excluding Achebe's other novels like *No Longer at Ease*, a work about the career of the grandson of Okonkwo, the protagonist of the earlier novel, as well as *Arrow of God* (the immediate sequel to *Things Fall Apart* but the third novel published). The subject of Achebe's growing self-referentiality, self-quotation and self-revaluation is one crying out for further investigation.

Even Achebe's fourth novel, *A Man of the People*, a work that takes his socio-political and cultural exploration up to the climactic events of the post-independence period of disillusionment, has carried over a lot from the style of its predecessors. But particularly significant is that in his latest book of fiction, *Anthills of the Savannah*, Achebe has returned with a vengeance not seen since his first novel to the oral base of his writing. Published 30 years after his novelistic debut, *Anthills of the Savannah* bears the marks of an anxious search for new modes of representation that could adequately document the legacy of military dictatorships in Africa, and while its subject matter may be dramatically remote from the concerns of the previous novels, the stylistic affinities it bears with them are unmistakable.

Things Fall Apart was published as written and no changes have ever been made to it; so the text has remained fixed and constant, giving critical commentary a stable material to work with, which is not the case with its direct sequel *Arrow of God*, first published in 1964 and revised in 1972. On the subject of adaptation, however, a little more can be said since one television series has been made out of the novel. Though it's not rendered as memorably as the text itself, which it often distorts in significant ways, the television version is full of interest. Chief among the areas of its appeal without question is the visuality, the ability to convey pictorially to an urban audience, who might have hitherto been unfamiliar with the surprisingly still-vibrant rural village life in Africa, the specificity, the flora and fauna of an Igbo rural setting.

An indigenous Nigerian Television Authority (NTA) production that first aired with tremendous fanfare over several weeks to a Nigerian national audience in 1986, *Things Fall Apart* (Television Miniseries), as it's titled, was scripted by Adiela Onyedibia and directed by David Orere, with a 13-part structure, each episode corresponding to a major sequence of the events narrated in the novel. If one sees the power of *Things Fall Apart*, in line with Achebe's conceptualization of the story, as residing in Okonkwo's blundering acts of recklessness that give ammunition to, rather than disarm, his opponents, one will be inclined toward being disappointed by the effect produced by the manner of the film's leading actor, Peter Edochie, who played Okonkwo's role with such a relish that it caused a certain re-alignment to the original tone of the novel by erasing the unappealing aspects assigned to Okonkwo's character; unlike the novel's protagonist who gains no understanding of his situation, is stern, and a bully, the film's Okonkwo is a warm and likable warrior, a sympathetic hero. However, the psychological neutralization does not completely ruin the story. Given the moderate resources involved (there are no elaborate scenes that are busy with movement, inventive music or special effects), the result must be gratifying for the producers. The film overall manages to recapture the subject matter of Achebe's novel with considerable verve: the European assault that broke up a pristine Igbo culture, especially the splash and colour of Igbo ritual events such as weddings, burial ceremonies, village-square oratory, and festival.

Despite giving the protagonist's character a new slant and a lack of ambitiousness in staging (the film has a static, unvarying setting that is frequently tiresome), to its credit the production impresses wholly by its force in capturing the intensity of Okonkwo's meteoric rise to eminence by dethroning the reigning wrestling title holder, his disconnection from both his father and his wives (in the opening episode, 'Footprints of a Tiger'). After the next two sections, respectively titled 'Crown of Battle' and 'Now or Never', concentrating on the frenzy of Okonkwo's efforts to prove himself as a leading warrior when his village is caught up in a war with a neighbouring village, and his diffidence in public debate when the elders of his Umofia community meet to present the case for war, Episode 4 ('The Choice') focuses on the Okonkwo-led delegation to Mbaino to exact retribution for the murder of a woman of Umofia. In Episode 5 ('One Boy, One Girl'), the boy hostage Ikemefuna arrives in Okonkwo's household; and Okonkwo's rashness shows when he beats second wife Ekwefi over her cutting of the leaves of a banana tree, an anger that resurfaces in Episode 6 ('A Tale of Two Clans'), where he beats his youngest wife Ojiugo during the Week of Peace and incurs the reprimand of Ani, the earth goddess.

With Okonkwo's participation in Ikemefuna's ritual murder taking centre stage in Episode 7 ('To Love and to Obey'), the ground is set for the protagonist's downfall, and Episode 8 ('Relief'), despite its misleading title, confirms this downturn of events with several ominious signs: the vehement opposition of Okonkwo's best friend Obierika over his actions, Okonkwo's own increasing mental torture, and his son Nwoye's growing disaffection. Not even the elaborate wedding of Obierika's daughter Akueke, at which he participates actively, can bring Okonkwo any personal comfort or relief.

Matters are then brought to an ugly head in Episode 9 ('New Times, New Tides'), which takes up the funeral rites of elder Ezeudu, where Okonkwo's gun accidentally discharges and kills the deceased man's son, leading to Okonkwo's being forced with his family into exile in Mbanta, his mother's home village. Correspondingly, the white man invades the territory in Episode 10 ('There They Come'), and begins to evangelize despite the opposition by Okonkwo, whose own son Nwoye converts to the new religion, the elaborate activities of which are subsequently taken up in the eleventh episode ('Gods and Gods') even as Okonkwo completes his mandatory exile, which is marked with a farewell party, and returns to his changed homeland of Umofia – the focus of the twelfth episode ('Home at Last') – finally murdering the leader of the British imperial army that has come to disperse a meeting Umofia has called to discuss the foreign presence in the final episode ('Here I Stand'), before taking his own life.

M. Keith Booker aptly observes that this film may have originally been designed for a Nigerian audience, but its usefulness is not limited to its local context of production. On the contrary, it should have 'considerable educational value for Western students of Achebe, who can use the series as an opportunity to help them visualize the unfamiliar cultural setting of the novel' (2003: 258). In this regard, it's helpful that the film is available on VHS from the African Video Centre in London. It will have to be admitted nevertheless that, even for the Nigerian audience, the impact of the project may not have been as hoped. If a prime objective of the producers was to use the project to expand an audience base for Achebe's novel, for example, then that goal may not have been significantly realized since it is the same spectrum of the literate public likely to have read the novel in print that also has access to television in Nigeria. But, not to take anything away from the spectacular significance that this pioneering effort to extend the afterlife of the novel beyond the print media represents, it should be acknowledged as well that by linking theatre and film to literature, the television production of Achebe's novel has inserted itself centrally as a vital part of the history of African culture which should be considered in any discussion of the transformation, dissemination or distribution, and transmission of texts and meanings in and across cultures.

STUDY QUESTIONS

1. This chapter has identified the variety of interpretive methods that critics have brought to bear in the reading of *Things Fall Apart* – for example, anthropology, biography, feminism, formalism, historicism, postcolonial theory, reader response, legal approach, Marxism, moral-philosophical apparatus. Which of these approaches do you find most compelling, and why?

2. To judge from the enthusiastic response, *Things Fall Apart* has warmed the hearts of readers in a way that few novels can boast of. What do you think are the reasons for the novel's undisputed universal appeal?

3. *Things Fall Apart* has been made into a reasonably successful serialized television drama and broadcast nationally in Nigeria, but how would you adapt it for the stage to attract an urban theatre audience? What would your key episodes be, and what types of actors and actresses would you use?

NOTES

CHAPTER 1: THE CONTEXTS OF ACHEBE'S WRITINGS

1. For excellent discussions of the cultural impact of colonization, see Michael Echeruo (1977); Oladele Taiwo (1976); and Emmanuel Obiechina (1975).
2. One will have to accept an observation James Olney made a long time ago that 'much of the best literature from Africa generally is – in a strict as well as in a loose sense of the word – autobiographical' (1972: 7).
3. Kofi Awoonor observed quite early the 'remarkable assimilation of African and European features' that 'not only brought into fiction in English an integrated African world, but also achieved the feat of presenting that world in its entirety in an unrelated language. Achebe's debt to the oral tradition is expressly in his creation of a new English style that follows and derives from his own Igbo African vernacular, idiom, rhythm, and tenor of speech. Above all, he exhibits a remarkable grasp of the proverb, which constitutes for the Igbo the "palm-oil with which words are eaten"'(1975: 251). And recent evaluation by eminent folklorist Isidore Okpewho extends this affirmation, describing the text as 'an unusual novel not only for the "strange" world it portrays but equally for the unfamiliar touch Achebe brings to the English medium of his writing' (2003: 39). The achievement of this novel, Okpewho restates, lies in initiating 'a vogue in postcolonial African literature whereby writers, while representing their societies in a European language, endeavored to create a space for their indigenous sensibilities in both sound (African words inserted here and there) and sense (peculiar ways of meaning)' (39).
4. One thinks immediately of the generation of playwright Femi Osofisan and poet Niyi Osundare, both of whom worked together at the University of Ibadan through the late 1970s to the early 1990s, but were rumoured not to have been on speaking terms all through their time together, in just about the way Bruce King says that Clark and Soyinka's relationship was to suffer a decline while they taught together later at the University of Lagos due to Clark's 'envy of Soyinka' (1993: 113).

CHAPTER 2: UNITY AND VARIETY IN STRUCTURE, LANGUAGE, STYLE AND FORM

1. This assessment of narrative technique in *Things Fall Apart* agrees with a statement Wayne C. Booth made long ago, that while 'narration is an art, not a science . . . this does not mean that we are necessarily doomed to fail when we attempt to formulate principles about it. There are systematic elements in every art, and criticism of fiction can never avoid the responsibility of trying to explain technical successes and failures by reference to general principles. But we must always ask where the general principles are to be found' (1983: 164). As Booth adds further, readers cannot legitimately legislate what artists must do, but they do have a right to point out what works well and what doesn't in a literary piece.

2. Despite the scantiness of attention devoted to this subject, there is a complete lack of unanimity of opinion about the identity of the narrator in *Things Fall Apart* among those who have given any thought to the matter at all. For example, Angela Smith refers to the 'omniscient' narrator and says, 'The central unifying and thought-provoking force of the novel is the narrator's voice, which weaves in and out of the characters' consciousness but retains an utterly distinctive quality not present in *Arrow of God* or in any other African novel depicting the clash of cultures in a rural setting' (1998: 23). But David Carroll reasons that 'The novel is narrated in the third person, but there is no suggestion of an omniscient narrator scrutinizing and analysing the customs and habits of this Igbo community. The voice is that of a wise and sympathetic elder of the tribe who has witnessed time and time again the cycle of the seasons and the accompanying rituals in the villages' (1990: 33). While Lynn Innes concurs that 'the narrative voice is primarily a recreation of the persona which is heard in the tales, history, proverbs and poetry belonging to the oral tradition' (1979: 111), and she is joined by Emmanuel Obiechina (1993: 133), Kenneth Harrow speaks of 'the narrator as a speaker of proverbs' and commends the use of 'distancing markers' that 'draw the audience closer to the teller of the tale than is the usual case with the realist novel' (1994: 114). However, Simon Gikandi questions entirely the usefulness of such assignments as searching for the identity of the narrator and contends that 'our concern should not be with the personality of this narrator, nor his/her identity; rather, our emphasis should be on how this narrator functions in the text and on his/her shifting focalization, the different perspectives "in terms of which the narrated situations are presented"' (1991a: 45), doubts which Alan Palmer rids us of, when he reiterates emphatically that 'the concept of focalization is crucially relevant to the study of fictional minds because it is concerned with the decisions that readers make about which consciousness is being presented in the text at any one time' (2004: 48).

3. It's surprising that critics have not yet given the importance of *Things Fall Apart*'s focalization the detailed focus it merits, though several passing references have been made to it. David Carroll alludes to this

matter when he speaks of the 'detached yet tolerant tone of the narrator' (1990: 35). Isidore Okpewho terms it a style that combines both an 'objective stance' and 'distance' as 'approaches' to aspects of Igbo culture (2003: 30–1). David Cook says 'Achebe is objective in *Things Fall Apart* not because he is indifferent – far from it; but because he is looking beneath the surface of things at the play of forces in historical context' (1977: 68). Yet Richard Begam states that the same element causes the reader to have 'difficulty establishing Achebe's position on a number of issues' (2002: 10). This is the point Wole Soyinka has in mind when he observes in Achebe's writing a neurotic striving for a symmetry of balance, objectivity, neutrality, omniscience and congruence, all of which he says fatally took the life out of the ideological thrust of the novelist's creative temper (1976: 12).

4. Francoise Lionnet is closer to the truth when she remarks about '[t]he message proclaimed by contemporary art and literature from Africa and the Caribbean' that 'It is not assimilation that is inevitable when Western technology and education are adopted by the colonized, or when migration to the metropole severs some of the migrants' ties to a particular birthplace. Rather, the move forces individuals to stand in relation to the past and the present at the same time, to look for creative means of incorporating useful "Western" tools, techniques, or strategies into their own cosmology or *Weltanschauung*' (1995: 11).

5. Chinua Achebe, *Things Fall Apart* (1958). Subsequent references are to this edition and are cited parenthetically in the text.

6. Achebe addressed the debate regarding the appropriate language of African literature in an essay entitled 'The African Writer and the English Language', in which he envisions 'a new voice coming out of Africa, speaking of African experience in a world-wide language'. This domesticated English language, he writes, must be one 'prepared to pay . . . submission to many different kinds of use'; a language able to 'bring out' the African writer's 'message best' without being altered 'to the extent that its value as a medium of international language will be lost' (1975: 100).

7. Ernest Emenyonu first initiated the movement to place Achebe's novels at the centre of what promised to be an extended discussion of orality and its appropriations by modern African writers, in his 1978 book, *The Rise of the Igbo Novel*. There, he argues that Achebe's novels, like all Igbo literature, originate from the oral tradition. However, he confines his discussion to a general outline of a key motif, 'the concept of the hero', in Pita Nwana's Igbo novel, *Omenuko*, the main model that Achebe is said to have had for *Things Fall Apart*. Thanks to him, the ground is now cleared for us to move forward. For his part, Emmanuel Egar addresses his study to disputing the claim that Africa did not have rhetoric, setting out to offer a comparative study of 'the social life of Umofia in *Things Fall Apart* with that of the Greek polis of the fifth and sixth centuries, and from that base, attempt to show a curious similarity in the use of rhetoric by two races, two cultures that never met in history' (2000: xvii). In a similar vein, Chinwe Okechukwu (2001), though also

an Igbo scholar – from the same village as Achebe, according to the fore-word to her book – who should have the range and experience to address the specifically Igbo contexts of his novel, does not take advantage of her ethnic background by focusing on this largely unexplored area. Instead, her plan is to help readers understand Achebe's art through the Greek notions of debate by analysing the rhetorical tropes.

CHAPTER 3: READING *THINGS FALL APART*

1. Although South African author Sol T. Plaatje's *Mhudi: An Epic of South African Native Life a Hundred Years Ago* (1930), a novel that incorporates oral tradition, biblical teachings and political commentary in presenting a cultural history of an indigeneous African group, is usually considered the first elegant work of realistic historical fiction written by a continen-tal African, its religious tone and didactic narrative style have not exer-cised a decisive influence on mainstream African fiction. It is notable that several works by other African authors exist in the genre of historical fiction, but *Things Fall Apart* establishes its difference quite clearly from all of them with its depth and breadth of perception in portraiture. The list is long and distinguished, and includes Camara Laye's *The African Child* (1955), Ngugi wa Thiong'o's *The River Between* (1965), Elechi Amadi's *The Concubine* (1966), John Munonye's *The Only Son* (1966), and Wole Soyinka's *Ake* (1981). *Things Fall Apart* lacks the narrow focus of either Laye's *The African Child* or Soyinka's *Ake*, for example, both of which are respectively preoccupied with the singular topics of nostalgic longing for a lost idyllic past and obsession with childhood and growing up; in contrast to the sentimental frame of those texts, *Things Fall Apart* has unique realistic styles and setting, a rich texture as well as a broad range. It is astonishing in that it combines a detailed pyschological pen-etration mapping tribulations in father–daughter and father–son rela-tionships with events of the public space, such as practices relating to judicial procedures and burial, along with brief but telling references to ritual behaviour and religious observance and the social organization of the Igbos, their patterns of kinship and male succession, extending the same illuminated descriptions to the account of the up to now insuffi-ciently told story of the tragic encounter with Europe.
2. Notable among these scholars are Abiola Irele, 1965: 25; Paula Berggren 1997: 497; Bernth Lindfors, 1968: 6; Gareth Griffiths, 1971: 89; Eustace Palmer, 1972: 53; Biodun Jeyifo, 1990: 62; Chinwe Christiana Okechukwu, 2001: 15.
3. See G. D. Killam, 1969: 24; Arthur Ravenscroft, 1969: 16; Charles Larson, 1972: 38–9; Eustace Palmer, 1972: 48; David Cook, 1977: 72; Nelson Wattie, 1979: 70; David Carroll, 1990: 35; Lewis Nkosi, 1981: 32; M. Keith Booker, 1998: 71; and Clement Okafor, 2002: 118.
4. Excellent discussions of uses of symbolism in *Things Fall Apart* abound in several important essays by Eldred D. Jones, Bu-Buakei Jabbi, Donald Weinstock and Cathy Ramadan among others (see Guide to Further Reading). For example, the main thrust of Jabbi's argument is that in

Things Fall Apart 'realistic details sometimes become symbolic without giving up their literal or physical bases; for surface fact is hardly ever completely sacrificed on the altar of symbolic propensity. His art is ever so concealed!' (1978: 140). Weinstock and Ramadan state, 'Achebe uses a blend of realistic and symbolic modes, with symbolism worked in so smoothly that it becomes an integral part of the realistic texture' (in Innes and Lindfors [eds], 1979: 127). But my focus on the symbolism of the wrestling contest is, I believe, an entirely new one.

5. In David Cook's view, 'Okonkwo is a hero in that he shows exceptional bravery, firmness, even greatness of soul. A hero is by definition an exceptional figure and so he does not simply embody the average virtues of his society in a fairly typical form; he is very far from being an Everyman' (1977: 66). Gerald Moore endorses this view, saying it is 'Obierika who really represents the more typical role. Okonkwo is more like a sort of super-Igbo; an exaggeration of certain qualities admired by his people, but at the expense of others which the rounded man is expected to possess' (1980: 127).

6. Chinua Achebe, *Things Fall Apart* (1958), p. 3. Subsequent references are to this edition and are cited parenthetically in the text.

7. For details on the capitalistic traits which earn the Igbos the reputation of being a highly enterprising and individualistic people, see especially the elaborate studies by G. T. Basden, 1938; C. D. Forde and G. I. Jones, 1950; and Victor C. Uchendu, 1965.

8. See Florence Stratton, 1994: 25–7; Martin Klein, 2000: 30.

9. Eskia Mphahlele's take on this matter is noteworthy. Arguing against the notion that Okonkwo's death signals the death of tradition, he says one cannot deny the violent challenge posed to 'the traditional communal structure of African society' by 'new ways of life – economics, centers of authority, education, all of which tend to pull the individual away from the communal center', but when 'tragedy befalls a character, the community is not ruined thereby' because of a built-in power to absorb the shock; hence when 'Okonkwo makes his exit by suicide . . . no-one outside the close family circle is shattered by the event. There is a group feeling around it, yes. But there is none of the theatrical tragedies like say the deaths of Hardy's Tess and Mayor of Casterbridge; of Conrad's Lord Jim; of Flaubert's Madame Bovary, like the deaths of so many other lonely characters that people much of Western fiction. There seems to be a contradiction here, but maybe because the main characters are rooted in a communal life, their tragedies are absorbed by the community' (1974: 254). This is precisely the point: the extent of the fragmentation of Okonkwo's community is indicated by the fact that it is so deep, collective resistance is completely inoperable.

10. Surprising as it may seem, even some critics have accepted the misconception that Unoka's life is worthless. Charles R. Larson states: 'In Igbo terms, his life was a failure; during his life his only distinction was the accumulation of many debts; and in a brief dramatic scene we are shown an incident from Unoka's past where a man who had loaned him money attempted to get it back' (1972: 33). Among the welter of critical

interpretations attempting to appraise the portrait of Unoka, Oladele Taiwo puts it best when he states that 'Unoka is not the worthless man that his son makes him out to be. He is an accomplished artist whose expertise is much sought after by other villages. The picture of him which comes through from the pages of the novel is one of almost unqualified approval. Given this situation, the critic is entitled to wonder why the only use made of Unoka in the novel is the negative motivation he provides for Okonkwo' (1976: 121). See also A. G. Stock (1979: 88).

11. In obvious reflection of real life, literature is filled with stories of orphans or abandoned children travelling circuitous and dangerous routes in attempts to recover lost parents (Henry Fielding's *Tom Jones* and Charles Dickens' *Bleak House* readily come to mind); it seems therefore somewhat paradoxical that a son as fortunate as Okonkwo to be living at home with a father, who is so loving into the bargain, would show such an absolute lack of appreciation of a father whom many would be eager to give up everything to have.

12. Arguing an alternative viewpoint that presents Okonkwo as a victim of his circumstance, Eustace Palmer states, 'Okonkwo is what his society has made of him, for his most conspicuous qualities are a response to the demands of his society. If he is plagued by fear of failure and of weakness it is because his society puts such a premium on success; if he is obsessed with status it is because his society is preoccupied with rank and prestige; if he is always itching to demonstrate his prowess in war it is because his society reveres bravery and courage, and measures success by the number of human heads a man has won; if he is contemptuous of weaker men it is because his society has conditioned him into despising cowards. Okonkwo is the personification of his society's values, and he is determined to succeed in this rat-race' (1972: 53). See also Oladele Taiwo (1976: 114) and Gerald Moore (1980: 127) for slight modifications of this view.

13. Discussions of portraits of women in Achebe's fiction are often influenced by preconceived notions that both gender bias and lack of talent generally prevent African male authors from creating authentic, convincing female characters. In line with such opinions, Achebe is specifically accused of placing women in subservient roles; fashioning women in motherhood roles; consigning them to menial domestic duties; or only giving them power as priestesses or as mythological figures. See, among others, the studies by James Olney (1972); Phanuel Egejuru (1982); Rhonda Cobham (1990); Florence Stratton (1994); Catherine Bicknell (1998); Obioma Nnaemeka (1998); Chioma Opara (1998); Martin Klein (2000). However, in her important ethnographic study of traditional Igbo women, Ifi Amadiume adduces enormous evidence to support the view that in traditional Igbo society women do not customarily question patriarchy or hanker for equality with their menfolk; rather they ask only for the right to occupy their own spaces, within which the women derive their greatest personal satisfaction as productive members of society. These spaces include both domestic and public domains such as the home and the market and ritual arenas as well as social occasions;

and cooking and cleaning are not roles women despise or take lightly. 'Women were also concerned with the welfare of the town. Decisions to contribute money for public works and repairs or for other services were taken at their meetings. In times of epidemics or great unrest, women consulted diviners for the well-being of *Nnobi*. If the dry season became too dry, hot and unbearable, the Women's Council met and contributed money for visiting the rain makers' (Amadiume, 1987: 66). Catherine Acholonu, another woman of Igbo origin, presents a similar view (1985). In light of the weight of confirmation from the research of those like Amadiume and Acholonu lend to the images of women portrayed in *Things Fall Apart*, it seems clear that critics who accuse Achebe of projecting disempowering images of women are applying Western standards of authority entirely remote and alien to the Igbos.

14. As a part of the elaborate safeguards the traditional Igbo society has devised for the marriage institution, suitors are offered many opportunities to review their feelings before rushing into a serious commitment of this nature. In particular, in addition to bearing the monetary costs of the marital union, the male suitor is given several chances to reconsider taking on the burden of a major life decision of this magnitude. These checks and balances are not always entirely shock-proof, as the bad marriage of Uzowulu and Mgbafo clearly shows, but their overall usefulness is beyond dispute.

15. It is the view of some critics that Okonkwo acts in the same spirit when he obeys an order from the Oracle of the Hills and the Caves and participates in the execution of Ikemefuna in defiance of advice from his loyal friend Obierika and then more insistently from the community elder Ezeudu. Damian Opata (1987) argues in particular that Okonkwo acts in response to his recognition of the gods' sovereignity, not wilfully, so he is not morally answerable for what he has done; as a man, he is merely an instrument for the purposes of the gods that must be fulfilled.

16. Based on this love practice alone, Phanuel Egejuru would seem to be right in observing that 'there is nothing so far in African literature to parallel love stories like, for instance, Tristan and Iseult, or Abelard and Heloise; nor do we have anything to liken to Romeo and Juliet, Manon Lescaut, Madame Bovary, and a host of other passionate love figures of European Literature' (1982: 83). Egejuru attributes the absence of the passionate love theme in African literature to the contrasting lifestyle and world-views of Africans and Westerners. She makes the claim that, while 'Love is seen . . . as very fundamental to the Western concept of self-fulfillment, and it is basic to intimate personal relationships . . . [to] an African, it is unthinkable for a man to abandon his ancestral home in pursuit of a woman in the name of love' (83). This of course ignores widespread expressions of the passionate love theme in oral literature of many African peoples, obviously not excluding the Igbos. See, for example, p'Bitek (1974), Okpewho (1985) and Kapteijns (1999).

17. Like most enforced removals from home, Okonkwo's exile in Mbanta is marked by emotional turbulence – moments of excruciating pain and longing that he tries hard to cover up. Thus 'he regretted every day of his

exile' despite the goodwill of his mother's kinsmen who 'had been very kind to him'. The naming of his children reflects this state of his mind: 'He called the first child born to him in exile Nneka – "Mother is Supreme" – out of politeness to his mother's kinsmen. But two years later when a son was born he called him Nwofia – "Begotten in the Wilderness"' (115).

18. By far the most compelling demonstration of the power of women in the society of the Igbos depicted in *Things Fall Apart* is the one which occurs in the scene where Chielo, priestess and oracle to Ani, abducts Ezinma and holds her hostage for hours in the caves and hills on a dark and lonely night. Despite the fact that second wife Ekwefi is extremely terrified to the point of being hysterical with the fear that she might lose her only child, and her husband Okonkwo is just as fearful for the safety of his favourite daughter, both of the panic-stricken parents are helpless to alter the course of events.

19. The popular opinion of the act is that it is indisputable proof of Okonkwo's brutality (e.g. Killam, 1969: 20; Obiechina, 1975: 213; Wren, 1980: 44; Carroll, 1990: 42–5; Taiwo, 1976: 118; Nnolim, 1977: 58; Brown (in Innes and Lindfors [eds], 1979: 32); Okpewho, 2003: 34–5), although we cannot discount the finely argued dissenting view of Damian Opata (1987), who says that the incident suggests the pre-eminent power of the gods and the capricious uses to which they put human beings.

20. Among these are critics such as Romanus Okey Muoneke (1994: 108–12); Neil ten Kortenaar (1991); and of course the many citizens of Umofia who, we are told in the novel, have begun to appreciate 'the trading store' built by the white man as well as the fact that 'for the first time palm-oil and kernel became things of great price, and much money flowed into Umofia' (Achebe, 1958: 126).

21. Even in arguing against the main premise outlined by Carroll about *Things Fall Apart*'s essential difference from the European fictional norm, Eustace Palmer unintentionally lends it confirmation when he states: 'Those who open this novel hoping to find a description of noble savagery where the tensions of modern Western society do not exist, are likely to be disappointed. Umofia society is proud, dignified, and stable, because it is governed by a complicated system of customs and traditions extending from birth, through marriage to death. It has its own legal, educational, religious, and hierarchical systems, and the conventions governing relations between the various generations are as elaborate as any to be found in a Jane Austen novel' (1972: 48–9).

GUIDE TO FURTHER READING

Copious background information on Achebe exists in such essay anthologies as Brian F. Cox (ed.), *African Writers* (New York: Charles Scribner's, 1997, two volumes), Puspa N. Parekh and Sigma Fatima Jagne (eds), *Postcolonial African Writers: A Bio-Bibliographical Sourcebook* (Westport, CT: Greenwood Press, 1998), and Isidore Okpewho (ed.), *Chinua Achebe's Things Fall Apart: A Casebook* (New York: Oxford University Press, 2003). But Ezenwa-Ohaeto's sweepingly exhaustive study, *Chinua Achebe: A Biography* (Oxford: James Currey, 1997), is now the most comprehensive biographical source.

A number of works have appeared that expand the scope of Achebe background study to include the cultural contexts of his fiction. The most stimulating of these is Robert Wren's *Achebe's World: The Historical and Cultural Context of the Novels* (Washington DC: Three Continents Press, 1980). An informed, lucid presentation of the contours of Igbo spirituality is Clayton G. Mackenzie's 'The Metamorphosis of Piety in Chinua Achebe's *Things Fall Apart*', *Research in African Literatures* 27 (1996): 128–38. An elaborate discussion of how colonial contact translated into a spiritual combat between the Igbo peoples and Europeans is Emmanuel Meziemadu Okoye's consistently interesting and concisely written, deeply pondered report, *The Traditional Religion and Its Encounter with Christianity in Chinua Achebe's Novels* (New York: Peter Lang, 1987), and comprehensive in its details is Kalu Ogbaa's ambitious and wide-ranging study of the theological integrity of Igbo, *Gods, Oracles and Divination* (Trenton, NJ: Africa World Press, 1992), and his large, attractive selection of anthropological, historical, religious and literary materials, *Understanding*

Things Fall Apart: A Student Casebook to Issues, Sources, and Historical Documents (Westport, CT: Greenwood Press, 1999), which is full of compact, thoughtful general reflections pertinent to a solid grasp of the novel. By far the most comprehensive listing of the major fictional characters, concepts, historical places and events, along with extensive reviews of earlier criticism, is M. Keith Booker's monumental edited volume, *Chinua Achebe Encyclopedia* (Westport, CT: Greenwood Press, 2003).

Eldred D. Jones's brief study 'Language and Theme in *Things Fall Apart*', *Review of English Literature* 5.4 (1964), 39–43, still remains the most insightful attempt to define the linguistic archaeology of this novel. Erudite image studies are Bu-Buakei Jabbi's 'Fire and Transition in *Things Fall Apart*', *Obsidian II* 1.3 (1975), 22–36 (reprinted in Innes and Lindfors [eds], 1979 and Okpewho, 2003) and Donald Weinstock and Cathy Ramadan's 'Symbolic structure in *Things Fall Apart*', *Critique* 11, 1 (1969): 33–41 (reprinted in Innes and Lindfors [eds], 1979). Good also on aesthetic devices are Solomon Iyasere's 'Narrative Techniques in *Things Fall Apart*', *New Letters* 40 (1974): 73–93; JanMohamed's 'Sophisticated Primitivism: The Syncretism of Oral and Literate Modes in Achebe's *Things Fall Apart*', *Ariel: A Review of International English Literature* 15 (1984): 19–39; Lekan Oyeleye's '*Things Fall Apart* Revisited: A Semantic and Stylistic Study', *African Literature Today* 17 (1991): 15–23; Angela Smith's 'The Mouth with Which to Tell of Their Suffering: The Role of the Narrator and Reader in Achebe's *Things Fall Apart*', *Commonwealth: Essays and Studies* 11,1 [1988]: 77–90 (reprinted in Iyasere [ed.], 1998, pp. 8–26); Eugene B. McCarthy's 'Rhythm and Narrative Method in Achebe's *Things Fall Apart*', *A Forum on Fiction* 18 (1985): 243–56 (reprinted in Iyasere [ed.], 1998); and Julian Washerman's 'The Sphinx and the Rough Beast: Linguistic Struggle in Chinua Achebe's *Things Fall Apart*', *The Mississippi Folklore Register* 16,2 (1982): 61–70 (reprinted in Iyasere [ed.], 1998).

Analytically sophisticated studies of the linguistic permutations of proverbial usage are Emmanuel Obiechina's 'Narrative Proverbs in the African Novel', *Research in African Literatures* 24. 4 (1993): 123–40; Kenneth Harrow's 'Flying without perching – metaphor, proverb, and gendered discourse', in *Thresholds of Change in African Literature: The Emergence of a Tradition* (Portsmouth: Heinemann, 1994); Richard Priebe's 'The proverb, Realism and Achebe: A Study of Ethical Consciousness', in *Myth, Realism and the West African*

Writer (Trenton: Africa World Press, 1988); Austin Shelton's 'The "Palm oil" of Language: Proverbs in Chinua Achebe's novels', *Modern Language Quarterly* 30,1 (1969): 86–111; and J. O. J. Nwachukwu-Agbada, 'Chinua Achebe's Literary Proverbs as Reflections of Igbo cultural and Philosophical Tenets', *Proverbium* 10 (1993): 215–35. All of these represent substantial improvements on B. Lindfors' now dated 'The Palm Oil with which Achebe's Words are Eaten', *African Literature Today* 1 (1968): 3–18.

The best book-length study offering a dependable thematic and stylistic overview of all Achebe's fiction, including *Things Fall Apart*, remains David Carroll's *Chinua Achebe* (London: Longman, 1970; revised 1980 and 1990). Lynn Innes' *Chinua Achebe* (Cambridge: Cambridge University Press, 1990) is an uncommonly readable survey of all of Achebe's creative works, including an outstanding chapter on *Things Fall Apart*, and Simon Gikandi's *Reading Chinua Achebe* (Oxford: James Currey, 1991) is a fascinating and profound theoretically-grounded reading of the fiction with a brief but superb exploration of the literary complexity of *Things Fall Apart*.

Discussions of *Things Fall Apart* as a historical novel abound. Excellent are Edna Aizenberg's 1991 essay comparing Achebe's novel with Guatemelan writer Miguel Angel Asturia's novel *Men of Maize*, 'The Third World Novel as Counter-history: *Things Fall Apart* and Asturias's *Men of Maize*', in Bernth Lindfors (ed.), *Approaches to Teaching Achebe's Things Fall Apart*, New York: Modern Language Association of America, pp. 85–90; Robert M. Wren's '*Things Fall Apart* in Its Time and Place', also in Lindfors (ed), 1991, pp. 38–44; and Dan S. Izevbaye's 'The Igbo as Exceptional Subjects: Fictionalizing an Abnormal Historical Situation', again in Lindfors (ed), 1991, pp. 45–51.

A stimulating feminist reading is Rhonda Cobham's 'Problems of gender and history in the Teaching of *Things Fall Apart*', *Matatu* 7 (1990): 25–39. Good also are Biodun Jeyifo's 'Okonkwo and his mother: *Things Fall Apart* and issues of gender', *Callaloo* 16, 4 (1993): 847–58; Florence Stratton's 'Gender on the agenda: Novels of the 1980s by Ngugi and Achebe', in her *Contemporary African Literature* (New York: Routledge, 1994); Catherine Bicknell's 'Achebe's Women: Mothers, Priestesses, and Young Urban Professionals', in Leonard A. Podis and Yakubu Saaka (eds), *Challenging Hierarchies: Issues and Themes in Colonial and Postcolonial African Literature* (New York: Peter Lang, 1998), pp.

125–36; Chioma Opara's 'From Stereotype to Individuality: Womanhood in Chinua Achebe's Novels', also in Podis and Saaka (eds), 1998, pp. 113–25; Obioma Nnaemeka's 'Gender Relations and Critical Mediation: From *Things Fall Apart* to *Anthills of the Savannah*', again in Podis and Saaka (eds), 1998, pp. 137–60; and Kwadwo Osei-Nyame's 'Chinua Achebe Writing Culture: Representations of Gender and Tradition in *Things Fall Apart*', *Research in African Literatures* 30, 2 (1999): 148–64.

Damian Opata's essay 'Eternal Sacred Order versus Conventional Wisdom', *Research in African Literatures* 18 (1987), 71–9 (reprinted in Okpewho [ed.], 2003), has so far remained the only attempt to join legal and ethical approaches in the interpretation of Achebe's works. This important study blazes the trail of exculpating Okonkwo from the overwhelming guilt to which he is condemned by critics for his role in the murder of his foster child Ikemefuna in *Things Fall Apart*. It raises issues which should open new vistas for our reading of other creative works both in the Achebe canon, specifically, and in the corpus of other African authors.

BIBLIOGRAPHY

WORKS BY ACHEBE

Achebe, Chinua (1958), *Things Fall Apart*. London: Heinemann.
——(1960), *No Longer at Ease*. London: Heinemann.
——(1962), *The Sacrificial Egg and Other Short Stories*. Onitsha: Etudo.
——(1964), *Arrow of God* (revised edition, 1974). London: Heinemann.
——(1966), *A Man of the People*. London: Heinemann.
——(1966), *Chike and the River*. London: Cambridge University Press.
——(1971), *Beware, Soul Brother: Poems*. Enugu: Nwankwo-Ifejika (revised and enlarged edition, London: Heinemann, 1972).
——(1972), *Girls at War and Other Stories*. London: Heinemann.
——(1972), *How the Leopard Got His Claws*. Enugu: Nwamife.
——(1975), *Morning Yet On Creation Day: Essays*. London: Heinemann.
——(1983), *The Trouble With Nigeria*. Enugu: Fourth Dimension.
——(1987), *Anthills of the Savannah*. London: Heinemann.
——(1988), *Hopes and Impediments: Selected Essays, 1965–87*. London: Heinemann.
——(2000), *Home and Exile*. New York: Oxford University Press.

SELECTED INTERVIEWS

Nwachukwu Agbada, J. O. J. (1990), 'A Conversation with Chinua Achebe', *Commonwealth: Essays and Studies*. 13.1: 117–24.
Ogbaa, K. (1981), 'Interview with Chinua Achebe', *Research in African Literatures* 12 (1), 1–13.

CRITICAL WORKS ON *THINGS FALL APART*

Adebayo, T. (1974), 'The past and the present in Chinua Achebe's novels'. *Ife African Studies* 1 (1), 66–84.
Begam, R. (2002), 'Achebe's sense of an ending: history and tragedy in *Things Fall Apart*', in H. Bloom (ed.), *Chinua Achebe's Things Fall Apart: Modern Critical Interpretations*. Philadelpia: Chelsea House Publishers, pp. 5–18.

Berggren, P. (ed.) (1997), *Teaching With the Norton Anthology: World Masterpieces. Expanded Edition Volume I – A Guide for Instructors*. New York: Norton, pp. 492–500.

Bicknell, C. (1998), 'Achebe's women: mothers, priestesses, and young urban professionals', in L. A. Podis and Y. Saaka (eds) (2001), *Challenging Hierarchies*. New York: Peter Lang, pp. 125–36.

Bloom, H. (ed.) (2002), *Chinua Achebe's Things Fall Apart: Modern Critical Interpretations*. Philadelphia: Chelsea House Publishers.

Booker, M. K. (1998), *The African Novel in English: An Introduction*. Portsmouth, NH: Heinemann.

Booker, M. K. (ed.) (2003), *Chinua Achebe Encyclopedia*. Westport, CT: Greenwood Press.

Brown, L. W. (1972), 'Cultural norms and modes of perception in Achebe's fiction'. *Research in African Literatures* 3, 21–35.

Carroll, D. (1990), *Chinua Achebe* (revised edition). London: Macmillan.

Cobham, R. (1990), 'Problems of gender and history in the teaching of *Things Fall Apart*', *Matatu* 7, 25–39.

——(1991), 'Making men and history: Achebe and the politics of revisionism', in B. Lindfors (ed.), *Approaches to teaching Things Fall Apart*. New York: Modern Language Association of America, pp. 91–100.

Davies, C. B. (1986), 'Motherhood in the works of male and female Igbo writers', in C. B. Davies and A. A. Graves (eds), *Ngambika: Studies of Women in African Literature*, pp. 241–56.

Echeruo, M. J. C. (1975), 'Chinua Achebe', in B. King and K. Ogungbesan (eds), *A Celebration of Black and African Writing*. Zaria and Ibadan: Ahmadu Bello University Press and Oxford University Press, pp. 150–63.

Egar, E. E. (2000), *The Rhetorical Implications of Chinua Achebe's Things Fall Apart*. Lanham: University Press of America.

Egudu, R. N. (1981), 'Achebe and the Igbo narrative tradition'. *Research in African Literatures* 12: 43–54.

Eko, E. (1975), 'Chinua Achebe and his critics: reception of his novels in English and American reviews'. *Studies in Black Literature* 6 (3): 14–20.

Elder, A. (1991), 'The paradoxical characterization of Okonkwo', in B. Lindfors (ed.), *Approaches to Teaching Things Fall Apart*. New York: Modern Language Association, 1991, 58–64.

Emenyonu, E. (1971), 'Ezeulu: The Night Mask Caught Abroad by Day', *Pan African Journal* 4: 407–19.

——(1990), 'Chinua Achebe's *Things Fall Apart*: a classic study in colonial diplomatic tactlessness', in K. H. Petersen and A. Rutherford (eds), *Chinua Achebe: A Celebration*. Portsmouth: Heinemann, pp. 83–8.

Enekwe, O. (1988), 'Chinua Achebe's short stories', in Y. Ogunbiyi (ed.), *Nigerian Literature 1700 to the Present: Volume Two*. Lagos: Guardian, 1988, pp. 38–42.

Ezenwa-Ohaeto (1997), *Chinua Achebe: A Biography*. Oxford: James Currey.

Gikandi, S. (1991a), 'Chinua Achebe and the signs of the times', in B. Lindfors (ed.), *Approaches to Teaching Things Fall Apart*. New York: Modern Langauage Association of America, pp. 25–30.

——(1991b), *Reading Chinua Achebe: Language and Ideology in Fiction*. London: James Currey.

Gowdah, H. H. (1973), 'The novels of Chinua Achebe'. *Literary Half-Yearly* 14 (2), 3–9.

Griffiths, G. (1971), 'Language and action in the novels of Chinua Achebe'. *African Literature Today* 5, 88–105.

Heywood, C. (1967), 'Surface and symbol in *Things Fall Apart*'. *Journal of the Nigerian English Studies Association* 2, 41–5.

Innes, C. L. (1979), 'Language, poetry and doctrine in *Things Fall Apart*', in C. L. Innes and B. Lindfors (eds), *Critical Perspectives on Chinua Achebe*. London: Heinemann, pp. 111–25.

——(1990), *Chinua Achebe*. Cambridge: Cambridge University Press, 1990.

Innes, C. L., and B. Lindfors (eds) (1979), *Critical Perspectives on Chinua Achebe*. Washington: Three Continents Press.

Irele, A. (1965), 'The tragic conflict in Achebe's novels'. *Black Orpheus* 17, 24–32.

Iyasere, S. (1974), 'Narrative Techniques in *Things Fall Apart*'. *New Left Review* 40 (3), 73–93.

——(1992), 'Okonkwo's participation in the killing of his son in Chinua Achebe's *Things Fall Apart*: a study in ignoble indecisiveness'. *College Language Association Journal* 35 (3), 303–15.

Iyasere, S. (ed.) (1998), *Understanding Things Fall Apart: Selected Essays and Criticism*. Troy, NY: The Whitston Publishing Company.

JanMohamed, A. (1984), 'Sophisticated primitivism: the syncretism of oral and literate modes in Achebe's *Things Fall Apart*', *Ariel: A Review of International English Literature* 15: 19–39.

Jeyifo, B. (1990), 'For Chinua Achebe: the resilience and the predicament of Obierika'. *Kunapipi* 12 (2), 51–70.

——(1993), 'Okonkwo and his mother: *Things Fall Apart* and issues of gender in the constitution of African postcolonial discourse'. *Callaloo* 16 (4), 847–58.

Jones, E. D. (1964), 'Language and theme in *Things Fall Apart*', *Review of English Literature* 5,4, 39–43.

Killam, G. D. (1969), *The Novels of Chinua Achebe*. New York: Africana Publishing Corporation.

Klein, M. (2000), 'Achebe's *Things Fall Apart*', in M. J. Hay (ed.), *African Novels in the Classroom*. Boulder: Lynne Reinner, pp. 25–35.

Kronenfeld, J. Z. (1975), 'The "communalistic" African and the "individualistic" Westerner: Some comments on misleading generalizations in western criticism of Soyinka and Achebe'. *Research in African Literatures* 6, 199–225.

Kuesgen, R. (1984), 'Conrad and Achebe: aspects of the novel'. *World Literature Written in English* 24, 27–33.

Lindfors, B. (1968), 'The palm oil with which Achebe's words are eaten'. *African Literature Today* 1, 3–18.

Lindfors, B. (ed.) (1991), *Approaches to Teaching Achebe's Things Fall Apart*. New York: Modern Language Association of America.

McCarthy, E. B. (1985), 'Rhythm and narrative method in Achebe's *Things Fall Apart*'. *A Forum on Fiction* 18, 243–56.

McDougal, R. (1986), 'Okonkwo's walk: the choreography of *Things Fall Apart*'. *World Literature Written in English* 26 (1), 24–33.

Mackenzie, C. G. (1996), 'The metamorphosis of piety in Chinua Achebe's *Things Fall Apart*', in *Research in African Literatures* 27, 128–38.

Maduka, C. T. (1987), 'African religious beliefs in literary imagination: ogbanje and abiku in Chinua Achebe, J. P. Clark and Wole Soyinka'. *The Journal of Commonwealth Literature* 22 (1), 17–23.

Meyers, J. (1969), 'Culture and history in *Things Fall Apart*'. *Critique: Studies in Modern Fiction* 11, 25–32.

Mphahele, E. (1974), *The African Image*. New York: Praeger.

Muoneke, R. O. (1994), *Art, Rebellion and Redemption: A Reading of the Novels of Chinua Achebe*. New York: Peter Lang.

Niven, A. (1991), 'Chinua Achebe and the possibility of modern tragedy', in K. H. Petersen and A. Rutherford (eds), *Chinua Achebe: A Celebration*. Portsmouth: Heinemann, pp. 41–50.

Njoku, B. (1984), *The Four Novels of Chinua Achebe: A Critical Study*. New York: Peter Lang.

Nnaemeka, O. (1998), 'Gender relations and critical mediation: from *Things Fall Apart* to *Anthills of the Savannah*', in L. A. Podis and Y. Saaka (eds), *Challenging Hierarchies: Issues and Themes in Colonial and Postcolonial African Literature*. New York: Peter Lang, pp. 137–60.

Nnolim, C. E. (1971), 'Achebe's *Things Fall Apart*: an Igbo national epic'. *Black Academy Review* 2.1/2: 55–60.

——(1983), 'Form and function of the folk tradition in Achebe's novels'. *Ariel* 14 (1983): 35–47.

——(1988), 'The sons of Achebe'. *Kriteria* 1 (1), 1–14.

Nwachukwu-Agbada, J. O. J. (1993), 'Chinua Achebe's literary proverbs as reflections of Igbo cultural and philosophical tenets', *Proverbium* 10: 215–35.

Nwahunanya, C. (1991), 'Social tragedy in Achebe's rural novels: a contrary view'. *Commonwealth Novel in English* 4 (1), 1–13.

Nwoga, D. I. (1964), 'The offended *chi*'. *Transition* 15, 5.

——(1971), 'The *chi*, individualism and Igbo religion'. *The Conch* 3 (2), 118–20.

Ogbaa, K. (1982), 'A cultural note on Okonkwo's suicide'. *Kunapipi* 3 (2), 126–34.

——(1992), *Gods, Oracles and Divination*. Trenton, NJ: Africa World Press.

——(1999), *Understanding Things Fall Apart: A Student Casebook to Issues, Sources, and Historical Documents*. Westport, CT: Greenwood Press.

Ogede, O. (2001), *Achebe and the Politics of Representation: from colonial conquest and occupation to post-independence disillusionment*. Trenton, NJ: Africa World Press.

Ogu, J. N. (1983), The concept of madness in Chinua Achebe's writings'. *Journal of Commonwealth Literature* 18. 1, 48–54.

Ogunsanwo, O. (1987), 'Transcending history: Achebe's triology'. *Neohelicon* 142, 127–37.

Ojinmah, U. (1991), *Chinua Achebe: New Perspectives*. Ibadan: Spectrum Books.

Okafor, C. (1981), 'A sense of history in the novels of Chinua Achebe'. *Journal of African Studies* 8, 50–63.

——(1989), 'Chinua Achebe: his novels and the environment'. *College Language Association Journal* 32 (4), 433–42.

——(2002), 'Igbo cosmology and the parameters of individual accomplishment in *Things Fall Apart*', in H. Bloom (ed.), *Modern Critical Interpretations: Chinua Achebe's Things Fall Apart*. Philadelphia: Chelsea House Publishers, pp. 113–24.

Okechukwu, C. C. (2001), *Achebe the Orator: The Art of Persuasion in Chinua Achebe's Novels*. Westport, CT: Greenwood Press.

Oko, Emelia A. (1974), 'The historical novel of Africa: a sociological approach to Achebe's *Things Fall Apart* and *Arrow of God'*. *Conch* 6 (1/2), 15–46.

Okoye, E. M. (1987), *The Traditional Religion and its Encounter with Christianity in Chinua Achebe's Novels*. New York: Peter Lang.

Okpewho, I. (ed.) (2003), *Chinua Achebe's Things Fall Apart: A Casebook*. New York: Oxford University Press.

Olney, J. (1971), 'The African novel in transition: Chinua Achebe'. *South Atlantic Quarterly* 70, 229–316.

——(1972), *Tell Me Africa: An Approach to African Literature*. Princeton: Princeton University Press.

Olorounto, S. B. (1986), 'The notion of conflict in Chinua Achebe's novels'. *Obsidian II: Black Literature in Review* 1 (3), 17–36.

Omotoso, K. (1996), *Achebe or Soyinka: A Study in Contrasts*. London: Hans Zell.

Opara, C. (1998), 'From Stereotype to Individuality: Womanhood in Chinua Achebe's Novels', in L. A. Podis and Y. Saaka (eds), *Challenging Hierarchies: Issues and Themes in Colonial and Postcolonial African Literature*. New York: Peter Lang, pp. 113–24.

Opata, D. U. (1987), 'Eternal sacred order versus conventional wisdom', *Research in African Literatures* 18: 71–9.

——(1989), 'The sudden end of alienation: a reconsideration of Okonkwo's suicide in Chinua Achebe's *Things Fall Apart'*. *Africana Marburgensia* 22 (2), 24–32.

——(1991), 'The structure of order and disorder in *Things Fall Apart'*. *Neohelicon* 18 (1), 73–87.

Osei-Nyame, K. (1999), 'Chinua Achebe writing culture: representations of gender and tradition in *Things Fall Apart'*. *Research in African Literatures* 30 (2), 148–64.

Owusu, K. (1991), 'The politics of interpretation: the novels of Chinua Achebe'. *Modern Fiction Studies* 37 (3), 459–70.

Oyelele, L. (1991), '*Things Fall Apart* revisited: a semantic and stylistic study', *African Literature Today* 17: 15–23.

Palmer, E. (1972), '*Things Fall Apart*', in *An Introduction to the African Novel*. London: Heinemann, pp. 48–63.

——(1979), 'Chinua Achebe: *Things Fall Apart, No Longer at Ease, A Man of the People*, and *Arrow of God*', in *The Growth of the African Novel*. London: Heinemann, pp. 63–101.

Peters, J. (1975), *A Dance of Masks: Senghor, Achebe, Soyinka*. Washington, DC: Three Continents Press.

Pieterse, C. and D. Munro (eds) (1978), *Protest and Conflict in African Literature*. London: Heinemann; New York: Africana Publishing.

Podis, L. A., and Y. Saaka (eds) (1998), *Challenging Hierarchies: Issues and Themes in Colonial and Postcolonial African Literature*. New York: Peter Lang.

Priebe, R. K. (1988), *Myth, Realism and the West African Writer*. Trenton, NJ: Africa World Press.

Quayson, A. (1994), 'Realism, criticism, and the disguises of both: a reading of Chinua Achebe's *Things Fall Apart* with an evaluation of the criticism relating to it'. *Research in African Literatures* 25, 4: 117–36 (reprinted in Okpewho, 2003).

Ravenscroft, A. (1969), *Chinua Achebe*. Harlow: Longman.

Scheub, H. (1970), 'When a man fails alone'. *Presence Africaine* 74, 61–89.

Serumaga, R. (1978), 'A mirror of integration: Chinua Achebe and James Ngugi', in C. Pieterse and D. Munro (eds), *Protest and Conflict in African Literature*. London: Heinemann, pp. 70–80.

Shelton, A. J. (1964), 'The offended *chi* in Achebe's novels', *Transition* 13: 36–7.

——(1969), 'The "palm-oil" of language: proverbs in Chinua Achebe's novels'. *Modern Language Quarterly* 30, 86–111.

Simola, R. (1995), *World views in Chinua Achebe's works*. New York: P. Lang.

Smith, A. (1988), 'The mouth with which to tell of their suffering: the role of the narrator and reader in Achebe's *Things Fall Apart*', *Commonwealth: Essays and Studies* 11.1: 77–90; reprinted in S. Iyasere (ed.) (1998), *Understanding Things Fall Apart: Selected Essays and Criticisms*, New York: The Whitson Publishing Company, pp. 8–26.

Stock, A. G. (1979), 'Yeats and Achebe', in C. L. Innes and B. Lindfors (eds), *Critical Perspectives on Chinua Achebe*. London: Heinemann, pp. 86–91.

Stratton, F. (1994), *Contemporary African Literature*. New York: Routledge.

ten Kortenaar, N. (1991), 'How the center is made to hold in *Things Fall Apart*', *English Studies in Canada* 17: 319–36.

——(1995), 'Beyond authenticity and creolization: reading Achebe writing culture'. *PMLA* 110 (January), 30–42.

Ummukwu, O. (1991), 'The anatomy of anti-colonial discourse: a revisionist Marxist study of Achebe's *Things Fall Apart*'. *Neohelicon* 18 (2), 317–36.

Washerman, J. (1982), 'The Sphinx and the Rough Beast: linguistic struggle in Chinua Achebe's *Things Fall Apart*', *The Mississippi Folklore Register* 16, 2: 61–70.

Wattie, N. (1979), 'The community as protagonist in the novels of Chinua Achebe and Witi Ihimaera', in D. Massa (ed.), *Individual and Community in Commonwealth Literature*. Malta: The University Press, pp. 69–74.

Weinstock, D., and C. Ramadan (1969), 'Symbolic structure in *Things Fall Apart*', in *Critique* 11, 1: 33–41.

Winters, M. (1981), 'An objective approach to Achebe's style'. *Research in African Literatures* 12, 55–68.

Wren, R. (1980), *Achebe's World: The Historical and Cultural Context of the Novels*. Washington, DC: Three Continents Press.

Yankson, K. (1990), *Chinua Achebe's Novels: A Socio-linguistic Perspective*. Uruowulu-Obosi: Pacific Publishers.

GENERAL WORKS

Abbott, P. H. (2002), *The Cambridge Introduction to Narrative*. Cambridge: Cambridge University Press.

Abrash, B. (1967), *Black African Literature in English since 1952: Works and Criticism*. New York: Johnson Reprint Corporation.

Acholonu, C. (1985), *The Spring's Last Drop*. Owerri: Totan Press.

Afigbo, A. E . (1972), *Warrant Chiefs: Indirect Rule in Southern Nigeria*. London: Longman.

Aidoo, A. A. (1965), *The Dilemma of a Ghost*. Harlow: Longman.

——(1970), *No Sweetness Here*. Harlow: Longman.

Amadi, E. (1966), *The Concubine*. London: Heinemann.

Amadiume, I. (1987), *Male daughters, female husbands: Gender and sex in an African Society*. London: Zed Books.

Anene, J. C. (1966), *Southern Nigeria in Transition 1885–1906*. Cambridge: Cambridge University Press.

Anozie, S. (1972), *Christopher Okigbo: Creative Rhetoric*. London: Evans Brothers.

——(1981), *Structural Models and African Poetics*. London: Routledge & Kegan Paul.

Arinze, A. F. (1975), 'Christianity and Igbo Culture', in E. N. Emenanjo and F. C. Ogbalu (eds), *Igbo Language and Culture*. Ibadan: Oxford University Press, pp. 181–97.

Asturias, M. A. (1975), *Men of Maize*. Trans. G. Martin. New York: Seymour Lawrence-Delacorte.

Atkins, K. E. (1993), *The Moon is Dead! Give Us Our Money! The Cultural Origins of an African Work Ethic, Natal South Africa, 1843–1900*. Portsmouth, NH: Heinemann.

Awoonor, K. (1975), *The Breast of the Earth: A Survey of the History, Culture and Literature of Africa South of the Sahara*. New York: NOK.

Basden, G. T. (1938), *Niger Ibos*. London: Seeley.

Boahen, A. (1987), *African Perspectives on Colonialism*. Baltimore: Johns Hopkins University Press.

Booth, J. (1981), *Writers and Politics in Nigeria*. London: Hodder & Stoughton.

Booth, W. C. (1983), *The Rhetoric of Fiction* (second edition). Chicago: The University of Chicago Press.

Cohn, D. (1999), *The Distinction of Fiction*. Baltimore, MD: John Hopkins University Press.

Conrad, J. (1910), *Heart of Darkness*. New York: Harper & Brothers.

Cook, D. (1977), *African Literature: A Critical View*. London: Longman.

Cox, B. F. (ed.) (1997), *African Writers* (2 vols). New York: Charles Scribner's.

Davies, C. B., and A. A. Graves (eds) (1986), *Ngambika: Studies of Women in African Literature*. Trenton, NJ: Africa World Press.

Dickens, C. (1948), *Bleak House*. London: Oxford University Press.

Duerden, D. (1975), *African Art and Literature: The Invisible Present*. London: Heinemann.

Echeruo, M. J. C. (1977), *Victorian Lagos: Aspects of Nineteenth Century Lagos Life*. London: Macmillan.

Egejuru, P. (1982), 'The Absence of the Passionate Love Theme in African Literature', in D. F. Dorsey, P. Egejuru, and S. H. Arnold (eds), *Design and Intent in African Literature*. Washington, DC: Three Continents Press, pp. 83–90.

Ekechi, F. K. (1972), *Missionary Enterprise and Rivalry in Igboland 1857–1914*. London: Frank Cass.

Ekwensi, C. (1954), *People of the City*. London: Dakers.

Emenyonu, E. N. (1978), *The Rise of the Igbo Novel*. Ibadan: Oxford University Press.

Fielding, H. (1887), *Tom Jones*. London: George Bell.

Finnegan, R. *Oral Literature in Africa*. London: Oxford University Press, 1970.

Forde, C. D., and G. I. Jones (1950), *The Ibo and Ibibio-Speaking Peoples of South-eastern Nigeria*. London: International African Institute.

Furlong, M. (1997), 'Introduction', *The Pilgrim's Progress*. Rockport, MA: Element.

Gakwandi, S. A. (1977), *The Novel and Contemporary Experience in Africa*. London: Heinemann.

Gikandi, S. (1987), *Reading the African Novel*. London: James Currey.

Goody, J. (1977), *The Domestication of the Savage Mind*. Cambridge: Cambridge University Press.

Hardy, T. (1974), *The Mayor of Casterbridge*. London: Macmillan.

Harrow, K. (1994), *Thresholds of Change in African Literature: The Emergence of a Tradition*. Portsmouth, NH: Heinemann.

Irele, A. (1981), *The African Experience in Literature and Ideology*. London: Heinemann.

——(2001), *The African Imagination*. New York: Oxford University Press.

Jameson, F. (1981), *The Political Unconscious: Narrative as a Socially Symbolic Act*. Ithaca, NY: Cornell University Press.

Kapteijns, L. (1999), *Women's Voices in a Man's World*. Portsmouth, NH: Heinemann.

Kerrigan, J. (1996), *Revenge Tragedy: Aeschylus to Armageddon*. Oxford: Oxford University Press.

Kershner, R. B. (1997), *The Twentieth-Century Novel: An Introduction*. Boston: Bedford Books.

King, B. (1993), Review of R. Wren, *Those Magical Years: The Making of Nigerian Literature at Ibadan*. *Ariel* 24 (4), 118–22.

Larson, C. (1972), *The Emergence of African Fiction*. London: Macmillan.

Laye, C. (1955), *The African Child*, trans. J. Kirkup. London: Collins/Fontana.

——(1956), *The Radiance of the King*, trans. J. Kirkup. London: Collins/Fontana.

Lindfors, B. (1973), *Folklore in Nigerian Literature*. New York: Africana.

Lionnet, F. (1995), *Postcolonial Representations*. Ithaca: Cornell University Press.

Luxon, T. H. (1995), *Literal Figures: Puritan Allegory and the Reformation Crisis in Representation*. Chicago: University of Chicago Press.

Maja-Pearce, A. (1992), *A Mask Dancing: Nigerian Novelists of the Eighties*. London: Hans Zell.

Mbembe, A. (2001), *On the Postcolony*. Berkeley: University of California Press.

Melville, H. (1851), *Moby-Dick* (reprint edition). New York: New American Library.

Mofolo, T. (1925), *Chaka*, trans. Daniel P. Kunene. London: Heinemann.

Moore, G. (1980), *Twelve African Writers*. London: Hutchinson.

Moses, M. V. (1995), *The Novel & the Globalization of Culture*. New York: Oxford University Press.

Munonye, J. (1966), *The Only Son*. London: Heinemann.

Ngara, E. (1982), *Stylistic Criticism and the African Novel*. London: Heinemann.

Ngugi, W. T. (1965), *The River Between*. London: Heinemann.

——(1967), *A Grain of Wheat*. London: Heinemann.

Nkosi, L. (1981), *Tasks and Masks: Themes and Styles of African Literature*. Harlow: Longman.

Nnolim, C. E. (1977), 'A source for *Arrow of God*'. *Research in African Literatures* 8, 1–26.

Obiechina, E. (1975), *Culture, Tradition and Society in the West African Novel*. Cambridge: Cambridge University Press.

——(1990), *Language and Theme in African Literature*. Washington, DC: Howard University Press, 1990.

——(1993), 'Narrative proverbs in the African novel', *Research in African Literatures* 24.4: 123–40.

Ogundipe-Leslie, M. (1995), 'The Bilingual to the Quintilingual Poet in Africa', in C. B. Davies and M. Ogundipe-Leslie (eds), *Moving Beyond Boundaries: Volume I*. New York: New York University Press, pp. 103–8.

Ogunyemi, C. O. (1996), *Africa Wo/Man Palava: The Nigerian Novel by Women*. Chicago: University of Chicago Press.

Okara, G. (1970), *The Voice*. London: Heinemann.

Okigbo, C. (1971), *Labyrinths with Paths of Thunder*. London: Heinemann.

Okonkwo, C. (1999), *Decolonization Agnostics in Postcolonial Fiction*. London: Macmillan.

Okpewho, I. (1983), *Myth in Africa: A Study of its Aesthetic and Cultural Relevance*. Cambridge: Cambridge University Press.

——(1985), *The Heritage of African Poetry*. London: Longman.

Ousmane, S. (1960), *Gods Bits of Wood*, trans. F. Price. London: Heinemann.

Oyono, F. (1956), *HouseBoy*, trans. John Reed. London: Heinemann.

——(1969), *The Old Man and the Medal*. London: Heinemann.

Palmer, A. (2004), *Fictional Minds*. Lincoln: University of Nebraska Press.

Parekh, P. N., and S. F. Jagne (eds) (1998), *Postcolonial African Writers: A Bio-Bibliographical Sourcebook*. Westport, CT: Greenwood Press.

p'Bitek, O. (1966), *Song of Lawino*. Nairobi: East African Publishing House.

——(1974), *Horn of My Love*. London: Heinemann.

Peters, J. A. (1978), *A Dance of Masks: Senghor, Achebe, Soyinka*. Washington, DC: Three Continents Press.

Plaatje, S. (1930), *Mhudi: An Epic of South African Native Life a Hundred Years Ago*. Alice, South Africa: Lovedale Press.

Povey, J. (1967), Introduction to B. Abrash, *Black African Literature in English since 1952: Works and Criticism*. Brenham, Texas: Prairie Hill Books.

Scholes, R. and R. Kellog (1966), *The Nature of Narrative*. New York: Oxford University Press.

Scott, J. C. (1992), *Domination and the Arts of Resistance: Hidden Transcripts*. New Haven: Yale University Press.

Smith, E. Y. (1986), 'Images of women in African Literature: some examples of inequality in the colonial period', in C. B. Davies and A. A. Graves (eds), *Ngambika: Studies of Women in African Literature*. Trenton, NJ: Africa World Press, pp. 27–44.

Soyinka, W. (1976), *Myth, Literature and the African World*. Cambridge: Cambridge University Press, 1976.

——(1981), *Ake: The Years of Childhood*. London: Rex Collings.

——(1985), 'The arts in Africa during the period of colonial rule', in A. A. Boahen (ed.), *General History of Africa VII*. London: Heinemann, pp. 539–64.

Spivak, G. C. (1999), *A Critique of Postcolonial Reason: Towards a History of the Vanishing Present*. Cambridge, MA: Harvard University Press.

Stratton, F. (1994), *Contemporary African Literature and the Politics of Gender*. New York and London: Routlege.

Taiwo, O. (1976), *Culture and the Nigerian Novel*. New York: St. Martin's.

Thomas, N. (1994), *Colonialism's Culture*. Princeton, NJ: Princeton University Press.

Todd, L. (1982), 'The English Language in West Africa', in R. W. Bailey and M. Gorlach (eds), *English as a World Language*. Ann Arbor: University of Michigan Press, pp. 281–305.

Tutuola, A. (1952), *The Palm-Wine Drinkard*. London: Faber and Faber.

Uchendu, V. C. (1965), *The Igbo of Southest Nigeria*. New York: Holt.

Wren, R. M. (1991), *Those Magical Years: The Making of Nigerian Literature at Ibadan: 1948–1966*. Boulder, CO: Lynne Rienner.

Yankah, K. (1989), *The Proverb in the Context of Akan Rhetoric: A Theory of the Proverb*. New York: Peter Lang.

Zabus, C. (1991), *The African Palimpsest: Indigenization of Language in the West African Europhone Novel*. Amsterdam and Atlanta, GA: Editions Rodopi.

Zell, H., C. Bundy and V. Coulon (eds) (1983), *A New Reader's Guide to African Literature*. London: Heinemann; New York: Africana.

INDEX